THE COMPLETE GUIDE TO
Classroom Centers

Hundreds of Ideas
That Really Work!

Written by Linda Holliman

Edited by Janet Bruno

Illustrated by Patty Briles

Project Director: Sue Lewis

 ©1996, Creative Teaching Press, Inc., Cypress, CA 90630

Table of Contents

Setting Up the Room

Center Activities 47

Reproducibles 127

Introduction

The purpose of this book is to support, encourage, and validate all teachers, no matter where you are in the process of using centers. If you are just beginning to use centers, you may want to keep this book close at hand to use as a guide. If you have been using centers on a limited basis, you may want to use this book as a reference to take that next step. If you are an "old timer," this book will validate what you have already been doing as well as give you many great new ideas that can make your life a little easier.

What is a center?

A center can mean different things to different people. Ideally, a center is an area of the classroom where a variety of hands-on materials and meaningful activities are available for children to choose. Since classroom space is often at a premium, a center can also be a desktop, a tub, or even a sack of materials. The main thing to remember is that centers should provide opportunities for children to be actively involved in learning and making choices in a variety of ways.

Creative Teaching Press

Why use centers?

The time you invest in implementing centers is worthwhile because of the many benefits for you and your students:

◆ Centers give you more time to interact with students.

◆ Centers give you the opportunity to meet the needs of individual students through flexible grouping and varied activities.

◆ Centers allow for different learning styles.

◆ Centers encourage positive behavior because students are actively involved and are allowed to make choices.

◆ Centers build self-concept as students experience success.

◆ Centers give kids the opportunity to
  • Explore, discover, and create.
  • Practice and apply skills.
  • Problem solve and use critical thinking skills.
  • Become more independent learners.
  • Collaborate with classmates.

What does a centers classroom look like?

A centers classroom is a busy place. Children are scattered throughout the room taking advantage of every available center space. Children may be working alone, with a partner, or in small groups. The teacher may be walking around the room observing, monitoring, adjusting, and evaluating by asking questions and making anecdotal records. She may be working with a small group of children or conferencing with one child. She isn't behind her desk; she too is actively involved in the learning process. A centers classroom isn't chaotic, and it isn't quiet. There is a BUZZ and a HUM. That's the sound of children learning.

Creative Teaching Press

Implementing Centers in Your Classroom

Planning for Centers

Why am I using centers?

How do I plan for centers?

In planning for centers you need to take a look at your philosophy and teaching style. You have to clarify your goals before you can set goals for your students. Ask yourself how you want to use centers in your classroom.

- ◆ Why am I using centers?

- ◆ What are my goals and objectives for centers?

- ◆ Are centers for enrichment, free time, or a part of my whole program?

- ◆ How will I schedule centers into the day?

- ◆ How many centers do I want or have space for?

- ◆ How many children do I want at a center?

- ◆ How structured do I want my centers to be?

Centers take careful thought and planning, especially in the beginning. One of the most important things for you to remember is: take your time and think it through! If you jump in too fast, you may get frustrated and feel like giving up. You need to give centers time. There definitely will be adjustments for both you and your students.

Creative Teaching Press

What kinds of centers should I have?

There are several different kinds of centers. You may want to use one type or a combination of the different kinds. Centers can be curriculum-oriented, such as math, science, or writing centers. Using this type of center makes it easy to plan and meet specific academic goals you have for students. After you introduce skills and concepts to the whole class, plan activities that will allow students to practice, apply, and extend these skills. For example, if one of your social studies goals is reading a map key, plan map-reading activities for the Social Studies Center.

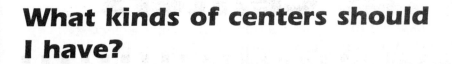

If you are using a thematic approach, you may want to develop theme-related activities for all the different curriculum centers. When studying an insect theme, create fantasy bugs in the Art Center, assemble insect collections in the Science Center, use bug manipulatives in the Math Center, etc. Another option is to have one ongoing Theme Center full of theme-related, integrated activities.

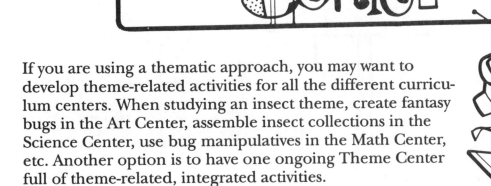

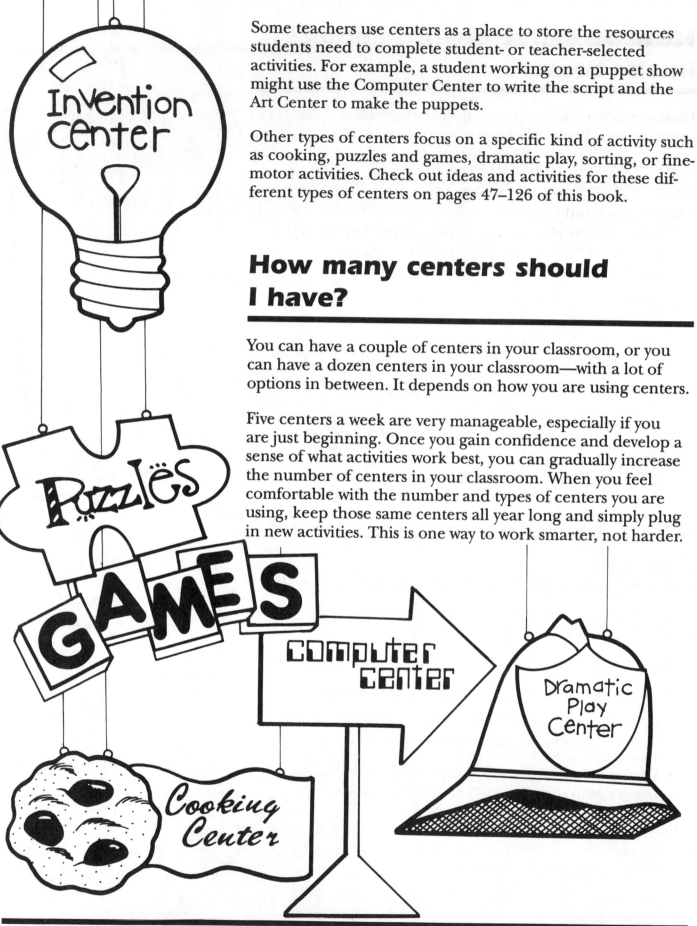

Some teachers use centers as a place to store the resources students need to complete student- or teacher-selected activities. For example, a student working on a puppet show might use the Computer Center to write the script and the Art Center to make the puppets.

Other types of centers focus on a specific kind of activity such as cooking, puzzles and games, dramatic play, sorting, or fine-motor activities. Check out ideas and activities for these different types of centers on pages 47–126 of this book.

How many centers should I have?

You can have a couple of centers in your classroom, or you can have a dozen centers in your classroom—with a lot of options in between. It depends on how you are using centers.

Five centers a week are very manageable, especially if you are just beginning. Once you gain confidence and develop a sense of what activities work best, you can gradually increase the number of centers in your classroom. When you feel comfortable with the number and types of centers you are using, keep those same centers all year long and simply plug in new activities. This is one way to work smarter, not harder.

How do I give children choices in the center?

Giving children choices is an important aspect of using centers. You can do this in a variety of ways

◆ Children can choose from a range of activities in the center.

◆ If there is only one activity in the center, children may choose how to respond to that activity (write a poem, design a poster, do an interview, make a book).

◆ Children can choose how to use the materials at a center. For example, materials at the Art Center can be used to illustrate a book, make a science poster, or make props for a play.

◆ Children can choose to work independently or collaborate with a classmate.

◆ Children can choose how long and involved each project will be.

What kinds of activities should I have?

As you begin to think about center activities, keep in mind these important guidelines:

◆ Center activities should be meaningful, not busy work.

◆ Center activities should be developmentally appropriate.

◆ Center activities should be multi-level and reflect the wide range of needs and abilities in your class.

◆ Center activities should be hands-on, providing the learner with opportunities for active involvement.

How do I develop appropriate activities?

Before you start developing your own activities, take a look at the sample activities on pages 47–117 of this book. This resource will help you get started and provide you with models for appropriate center activities. As you start to develop activities on your own, follow these simple steps:

1. Look at your state and local curriculum guides to determine what concepts and skills you are required to teach.

2. Create a checklist of skills and concepts that will allow you to monitor how children are progressing through the curriculum.

3. Make a list of the types of centers you have in your classroom, and look at the skills and concepts that apply to each of those centers.

4. Develop activities and materials that will allow children to practice and apply skills and concepts you have already introduced to the class.

5. Develop hands-on materials and activities that actively involve students.

Get kids actively involved.

Creative Teaching Press

The Center Activity Planning Sheet on page 128 will help you in this planning process. Complete this form for each center activity. As you observe children working at the center, use the form to evaluate the activity. How did the children like the activity? Was it too hard or too easy? Did the activity meet the goals and objectives as well as you thought it would? Include any suggestions for revisions or additions.

Develop a file for each center, and keep these forms in the file. You may also want to add photos of the center showing students working on the activities. The file will be a valuable reference when you are planning centers the following year. It also serves as an important accountability tool. When a parent or administrator questions why you're using centers or what "real learning" is taking place, pull out the file and show them!

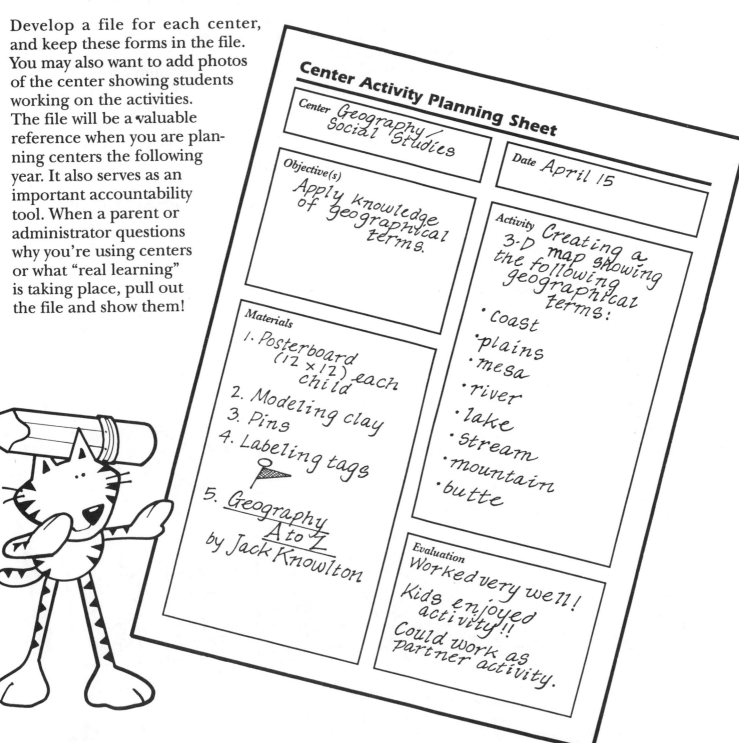

Center Activity Planning Sheet

Center *Geography/ Social Studies*

Date *April 15*

Objective(s) *Apply knowledge of geographical terms.*

Activity *Creating a 3-D map showing the following geographical terms:*
- *coast*
- *plains*
- *mesa*
- *river*
- *lake*
- *stream*
- *mountain*
- *butte*

Materials
1. Posterboard (12 × 12) each child
2. Modeling clay
3. Pins
4. Labeling tags
5. Geography A to Z by Jack Knowlton

Evaluation *Worked very well! Kids enjoyed activity!! Could work as partner activity.*

How will students know how to do the activities?

Students may already be familiar with many activities because you will have worked on similar activities in a large-group setting. Some center activities will be ongoing and will not need additional explanation. However, always model new activities. In addition, you may need to provide students with written directions.

You can write directions on a chart and post the chart at the center, or you can reproduce individual copies of the directions, which can be kept at the center. Any directions for young students and beginning readers should include illustrations showing how to complete each step. (See page 130 for some basic pictures to use in creating illustrated directions.) It's also helpful to post samples of some types of projects.

♥ Make Valentine ♥ Cards

1. Fold your paper.
2. Think about your design.
3. Cut ♥ ♥.
4. Glue on and ribbon.
5. Write your Valentine message.

Write an Acrostic Poem

1. Write your name down the side of the paper.
2. Begin each line with a letter in your name.
3. Illustrate.

Jumpin' Joey
Of Australia
Everyone knows
You're a baby kangaroo

How do I get enough materials?

cooking center

The first step is to inventory what you already have. Look in closets, storage boxes, and on shelves. Check in the teacher's room and in the basement. Borrow materials from colleagues and offer to share yours.

Make a wish list for parents. Include inexpensive items or materials they may already have around the house such as games and puzzles, lunch bags, magazines, or plastic containers. Ask parents to donate the gift of time to cut out laminated materials, do grocery shopping for the Cooking Center, or gather wood scraps for the Construction Center.

If you need to purchase materials, use your classroom allotment to buy consumables. Spend your own money on materials that you will use for a long time. That way you can take them with you if you move to another school or grade level. To extend your dollars, buy books, games, furniture, etc. at garage sales and thrift shops.

Think about organizing a "Centers Support-and-Share Group." Invite teachers in your building or district to join. The opportunity to share ideas, materials, successes, and failures will keep all of you going.

Dear Parents,

Please look around the house and see if you could donate any of the following items for our center time:
- magazines
- puzzles
- educational games
- plastic containers
- blank tapes

Sincerely,
Mrs. Holliman

Scheduling Center Time

■ ■

How much time should I allow for centers?

If you are just starting, you may want to have centers for only thirty minutes in the afternoon, or you may have children go to centers when they finish their assigned activities. If you are using a reading/writing workshop approach, incorporate centers into your activity time.

As you gain experience, you may begin to view centers as an integral part of your program and include them in the morning, the afternoon, or throughout the day. One possibility is to have a short instructional time with the whole class in the morning and again in the afternoon. The rest of the day, students move through centers according to their planning sheets, an assignment board, or a rotation chart. Some activities are assigned and others are self-selected, but students work at their own pace as they accomplish those tasks. While students work, the teacher observes, monitors, and conferences individual students or works with small groups on skill instruction, remediation, or enrichment activities.

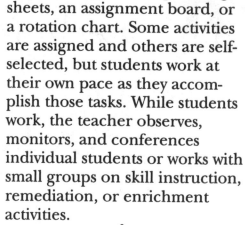

How should center time be spent?

Each center time should be composed of three sections—a focus time, a work time, and a sharing time. The first section is whole group and should be no longer than five minutes. This is an opportunity for you to remind children of procedures and help them focus on the work they will be involved in. You can review activity directions, discuss questions and concerns about activities or behavior, introduce a new activity, or reinforce the good work that you have observed at centers.

The largest section of time is for students to be actively involved in center activities. The length of time will depend on the time of year, the age of your students, and the types of activities. At the beginning of the year, students might spend 10–15 minutes in a center, but you can gradually lengthen the time throughout the year. Monitor your own class and make adjustments. If things get chaotic after 20 minutes, then keep center time short and increase it gradually.

As a general rule, younger children will be able to attend for shorter periods of time, but the type of activity is also a factor. Reading books at the Reading Center probably won't keep a kindergarten child engaged for 15 minutes, so you may want to add books on tape for that age level. The Block Center, on the other hand, could be in use for an hour, and they will beg for just five more minutes. Third graders may be content to read for 30 minutes and might sail through a science experiment in 15 minutes. You have to take all of these factors into consideration.

The length of the work time will also be affected by how you schedule children into centers. If you use a rotation system, the work time might be 60 minutes. If you use a self-selected system, the work time could last all morning, or throughout the day. (See pages 22–30 for a description of rotation and self-selected systems.)

The last 5–10 minutes should provide closure. You can point out positive center-time events or go over center rules, reminding children of correct procedures. Several students can share about what they did at centers. One child might read an original story or poem. Another might tell about a science experiment or show a painting created at the Art Center. You may want to provide a sharing sign-up sheet for children as this becomes a very popular part of the day.

What if students finish too fast or don't finish at all?

What to do with those who finish too soon or those who never finish is always a problem. You will probably notice a pattern. Miguel and Stephanie always finish first, and Tom and Alana never finish anything. This a fact of life, not a fact of centers. There are some steps you can take to remedy this problem.

◆ Set high expectations for center work, just like everything else in your classroom. Let children know immediately that you don't accept work that is done haphazardly.

◆ Adjust the activity for the child who has difficulty finishing.

◆ Consider putting the "tortoise and the hare" together as center partners and see if that combination can help both children.

◆ Provide a basket of books, mini-puzzles, or other small activites for those children who finish fast.

◆ Remember that some centers will have many choices so there shouldn't be a problem with fast or slow workers because of the available options.

The more you plan and prepare activities for the different types of centers, the better you will get at judging the amount of time it will take for children to complete the task. Sometimes you "hit" and sometimes you "miss." Give yourself permission to make mistakes and use it as a learning experience.

Preparing the Students

How do I group students for centers?

If you use a rotation system, you will need to group students. You will usually group them heterogenously, but there certainly is a time and place to have children with similar needs and abilities work together. For example, you can form groups for skill instruction or enrichment activities. Students can also work together on projects of common interest.

Groups don't have to stay the same and shouldn't. Changing groups weekly or monthly gives children the opportunity to work and interact with all class members. Since groups will be changing, it is important to post lists of the groups so students won't keep asking you, "What group am I in?"

You can assign each group a number, a color, a shape, or even a theme symbol. For example, if you are studying planets, you could give each group the name of a planet. Some of the rotation system charts on pages 24 and 25 list each child individually. On those charts, children can tell at a glance where they should be.

Creative Teaching Press

How many children should be at a center at one time?

One child may be at a center, or five children may be at a center. Once again, this is a personal decision. Some teachers feel that there should be at least two children so there can be interaction and collaboration. Others feel that being at a center alone allows for think-time and reflection.

You will need to consider the amount of space at the center as well as the number of activities available. The number of children in each center also depends on the type of management system used. These systems are discussed on pages 22–32.

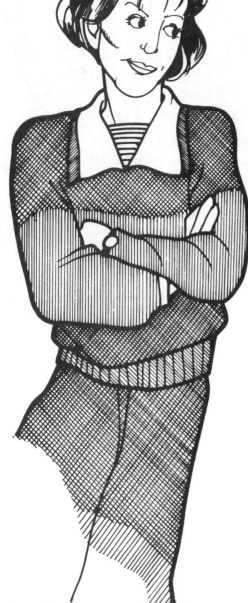

How do I schedule children into centers?

There are two basic choices for scheduling children into centers, a rotation system or a self-selected system.

Rotation System

When using a rotation system, children move through centers in a very systematic way. The use of a rotation wheel or chart is necessary. You will probably have a specific amount of time allotted for each center. Students work in the center for the specified time and then move on to another activity.

Self-Selected System

When using a self-selected system, children move themselves through the centers in a systematic way. The use of individual contracts or planning sheets is necessary to have a record of what centers the child is using and what activities have been completed.

Choose whichever system is most comfortable for you and your class. If you are just beginning or if your students are very young, you may want to start out with a rotation system because it provides more structure. As students develop more independence, you may want to change to a self-selected system. How you use centers with children can also vary from year to year. What works for one class may not work for a different group of children. You are the best judge of what works for your students.

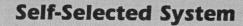

Creative Teaching Press

How does a rotation system work?

There are many ways to move students through centers on a rotation system. Five different systems are described below:

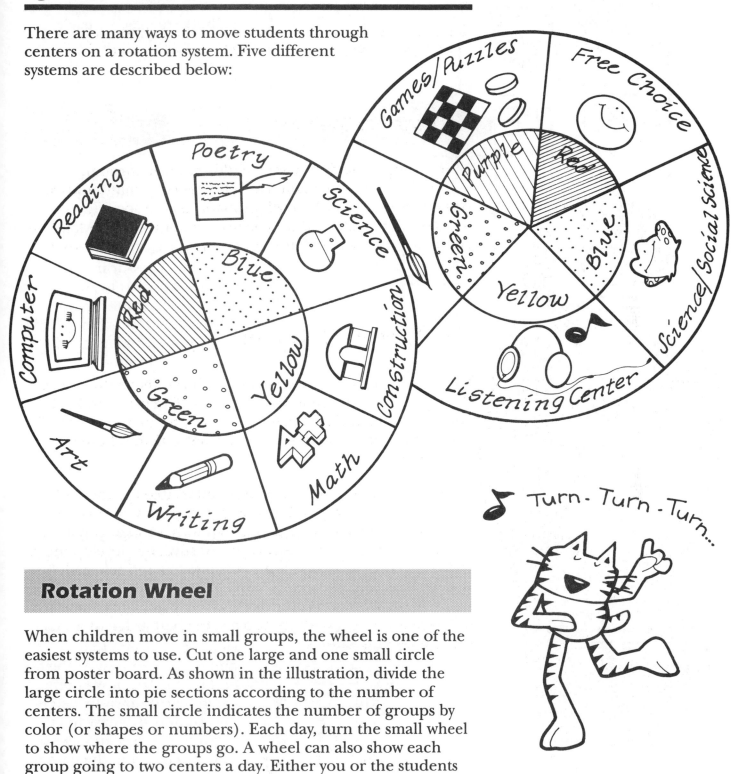

Rotation Wheel

When children move in small groups, the wheel is one of the easiest systems to use. Cut one large and one small circle from poster board. As shown in the illustration, divide the large circle into pie sections according to the number of centers. The small circle indicates the number of groups by color (or shapes or numbers). Each day, turn the small wheel to show where the groups go. A wheel can also show each group going to two centers a day. Either you or the students can choose which center to go to first.

Poster Board Chart

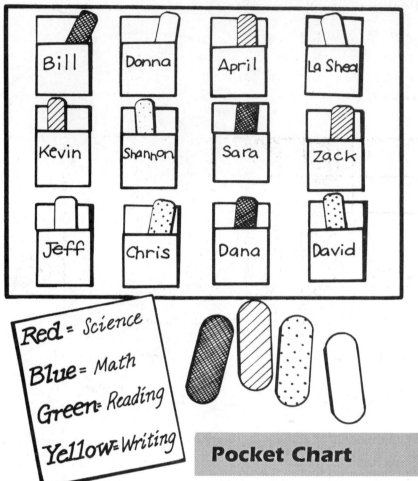

Red = Science
Blue = Math
Green = Reading
Yellow = Writing

For this chart you need a library pocket for each child, tongue depressors, and a large piece of poster board. Write each child's name on a pocket, and glue the pockets onto the board. Spray-paint the tongue depressors to color-code them for each center. For example, a red tongue depressor can indicate the Science Center. Each day or week, place a colored tongue depressor in every student's pocket to show them which center to use. This system offers flexibility in grouping students and varying the number at each center.

Pocket Chart

Using a pocket chart for the rotation system allows for flexibility in grouping. Write the center names and student names on sentence strips and laminate. (In kindergarten you can use rebus symbols for the centers.) Place the center names down the left side of the chart. Place student name cards by each center.

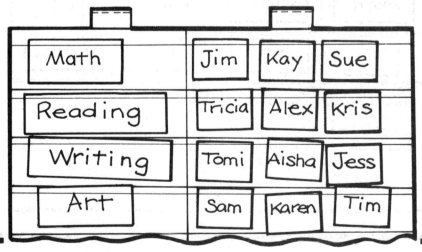

The pocket chart works best when students go to only one center per day. At the end of the day, move the center cards down to assign new centers. It's easy to regroup children at any time by changing the name cards.

Magnetic Board

Photocopy each child's school picture, laminate it, and put magnetic tape on the back. (As an alternative you can make a name card for each child.) On the magnetic board, make a grid with colored masking tape or markers to show the center options. This system also works using Velcro or hooks instead of a magnetic board and tape. The magnetic board is used just like the pocket chart.

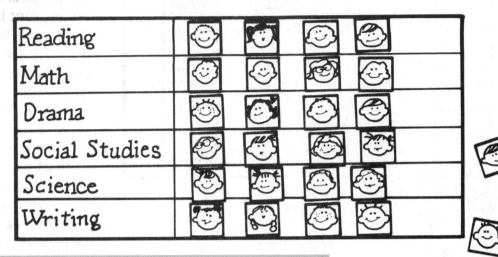

Planning Board

The planning board is a great system to transition children from a formal rotation system to a self-selected system. Use a magnetic board as described above; Velcro and hooks work too. The grid at the top of the board lists the groups and the four centers each group must visit that day. A "Choose" symbol indicates that students in the group may select from any of the day's center choices listed at the bottom of the board. In this way, students can start taking responsibility for their choices.

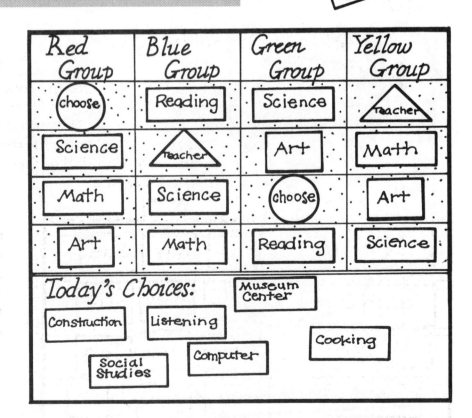

How does a self-selected system work?

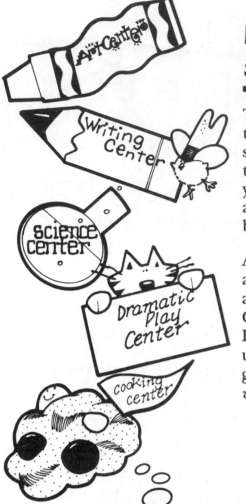

The main difference between the self-selected system and the rotation system is that children choose their centers and schedule when they will visit each center. Giving students that amount of choice might make you nervous. Don't worry; you created the centers and developed appropriate center activities, so everything students are choosing should be good!

A self-selected system can also be a combination of teacher- and student-planning. You can designate certain centers or activities as mandatory, such as Math, Reading, and Writing Centers, while students can choose other centers or activities. It's wise to periodically conference with students about their use of centers. Conferencing gives you the opportunity to guide children where they *need* to go as well as where they *want* to go.

The advantages of the self-selected system are many:

◆ Allows for more choice and fosters development of good decision-making skills.

◆ Gives students more responsibility for managing their time.

◆ Allows students to work at their own pace and provides for individual differences.

◆ Provides more time for students to pursue special interests and work on in-depth projects.

◆ Allows you to spend more time observing, monitoring, and conferencing with individual children or small groups.

◆ Provides you with more flexibility for grouping.

How do I control the number of children in each center?

Controlling the number of children in each center is critical for the success of self-selected centers. You need to be able limit the number of students at a center without having to personally monitor all the time. This can be accomplished in several ways.

Pocket Planner

Make a chart, similar to the one shown, with poster board and library pockets. Write the center name and the number of children allowed in the center on the front of each pocket. Write each child's name on a tongue depressor. As children make choices, they put their name in the correct pocket. When the number of tongue depressors matches the number on the library pocket, the center is full.

Cans and Clothespins

Clip clothespins on the top of the can to indicate how many children can work in that center. When a student goes into the center, he or she removes a clothespin and drops it in the can. The child replaces the clothespin when leaving the center.

Chairs

Put a particular number of chairs at a table to represent the number of children who can work at that center.

Stop and Go

Laminate red and green paper circles back to back. Punch a hole at the top and hang the appropriate number of "stoplights" at the center. Start all the circles on green. As children come to the center, they turn the light to red. When all lights are red, the center is full.

Center Necklaces

Make simple necklaces labeled with the center names. Hang them in a central location. Students take the appropriate necklace and wear it while in the center. When all the necklaces for one center are gone, children know it is full.

Creative Teaching Press

How can I track students' center choices?

When a self-selected system is used, it's important for you and your students to have a way to keep track of center choices. This can be done by using forms like those described below.

Color It In

The Color-It-In system is a very simple way to monitor what centers students are choosing. Prepare a form such as the one shown. Write in the names (or draw pictures) of centers in your classroom. As children work in the centers, they color in the circle to show where they have been.

Punch It Out

On a strip of paper, draw one circle for each center in your classroom. Number centers to correspond to the numbers on the punch-out card. Place a hole punch at each center. As children choose a center, they punch out the number to indicate they have completed the activities.

Planning Forms

Planning forms, contracts, and checklists give students the opportunity to plan on a daily basis, and each can be used in several ways. You can customize a planning form to match the centers in your classroom.

In examples A and B, the teacher fills in the center choices for the week and reproduces a copy for each student. Each day, students choose several centers to visit and mark them on the sheet. To add more structure, the teacher can check off required centers in one color, and the children can check their choices in another color. This can be done for the class as a whole or on an individual basis.

In example C, students write in their choices each day from a list posted in the classroom. Or the teacher can write in a few required centers such as Math, Writing, and Reading, and students can select additional centers from the list of center options for that week.

Example A

Example B

Example C

Creative Teaching Press

How will I know what students are doing at centers?

You need to have a way of keeping track of what activities students are involved with at the centers. And you need to be very specific about which activities are required, which are choices, and where and when you want finished work turned in. Center folders, center boxes, and activity menus are excellent tools to help students keep track of activity choices, finished products, and ongoing projects.

Center Folders

Every child should have a two-pocket folder which is kept in a box or tub in a central location in the classroom. If you are using a self-selected system, place the planning sheet, checklist, or contract in the left-hand side of the folder. Keep ongoing projects or finished products in the right-hand side of the folder. Separate folders for each child are very useful for tracking individual progress.

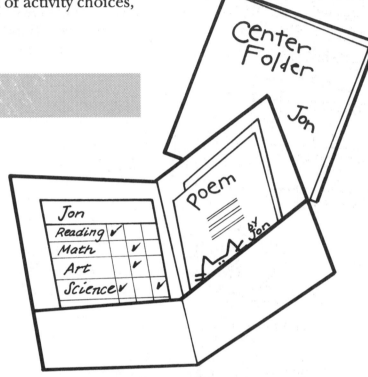

Center Boxes

If your students do lots of projects that won't fit into a folder, such as art projects, posters, and original books, consider providing each child with a box. Transparent plastic boxes with snap-on lids work especially well. They are not too expensive and can be used from year to year. Center folders will also fit into the box.

Have students stack the boxes by tables or center groups. You can tell at a glance which boxes are empty or nearly empty. Every Friday, empty the boxes; save some work for portfolios, and send the rest home. Place unfinished projects back in the box.

Science Menu
Rod

Egg Carton Insect	Ant Farm Activity	Research one Insect
Insect Collection	Life Cycle of Butterfly	Build a Fantasy Insect

Example A

Social Studies Menu
Fran 4/1

Complete 5 Activities

Map Activity	Read
Work on Pyramid	Mexican Holidays
Listen to Mexico tape	Aztec Mask
Cooking Activity	Help with Piñata

Example B

Activity Menus

If you have several activity choices at each center, it is a good idea to use activity menus. You need a separate menu for each center. Have students keep their menus in the center folders and boxes described on page 31. Examples of menus are shown on this page.

Example A is a simple grid that lists the activity choices at the center. As students complete each activity, they X out, color in, or write the date in the appropriate square. Or the teacher may initial the square after the student completes the task.

For example B, the child must choose a required number of activities from a menu of many possible choices. For example, the student might be required to complete six out of twelve possible choices. As the student completes each activity, he or she initials, colors, or writes the date in the square.

Example C works well if you keep your center activities in numbered containers. Divide the menu into squares to correspond with the number of activities at that center. As children work through each activity, they color in the square that matches the number of the activity.

Math Menu
chris

1	2	3
4	5	6
7	8	9

Example C

How can I prepare students to guarantee successful center experiences?

You've prepared the room, you've developed the activities, now it's time to prepare the students. This is the most critical factor for guaranteeing success. In the first few weeks, you need to model the procedures you've established and have your students practice, practice, practice! This training period usually takes a couple of weeks, but adjust the time to the needs of your class. It's better to spend extra time making sure students are using the centers in an acceptable way and are totally comfortable with the centers process.

1. Introduce the centers.

Take the children around the room and introduce each of the centers in a general way. Your enthusiasm in the introduction of the centers will be contagious. Try to involve your students. Ask them, "What would you like to do in the center? What materials would you like to have available? Do you have any activity ideas?" This orientation may take one day, several days, or a week depending on several factors: how many centers you have, the age of your students, and their previous experiences with centers.

2. Introduce the management system.

Whatever system you use—rotation or self-selected—you need to spend time with the children modeling how it works. Modeling is a critical part of the orientation process. No matter how simple a chart, wheel, or contract may seem, don't assume anything with your children. Go over the process in detail.

3. Practice the management system.

The centers are set up, the children know the system—now they need to practice using the system again and again and again until they understand it backwards and forwards. For example, if you are using a rotation wheel, have students look at the wheel to find their center, proceed to their center, return to their desks, proceed to the next center, etc. Students need to practice this for a couple of days.

If you are using a self-selected system, send a few children at a time to make their choices. Everyone will get to the centers in a few minutes, and there will be a smooth transition. As students rehearse, begin working on noise level in the centers. It will be noisy, but you need to train children that "up and around" does not mean "loud and out of control."

4. Practice using the activities.

During the next stage, students go to the center, take out activities, work with them correctly, and put them away correctly. For these rehearsals, provide simple activities that require no teacher direction. This practice may take several days to a week.

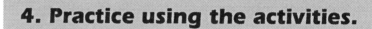

The first few weeks of centers, don't plan activities that require teacher involvement such as working with a small group or conferencing with students. You need to be up walking around, reinforcing, and monitoring center procedures, activities, and behavior. Your presence in this beginning stage is a crucial factor for success. To maintain standards, you will need to continue to monitor throughout the school year.

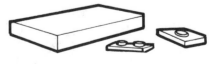

5. Practice the help procedures.

You need to establish procedures for how students get help when the teacher is not available. Will they write their name in a designated place in the room? Will you teach them the tried-and-true "Ask Three, Then Me" method, or will you have center captains available to help with general questions? Whatever procedure you establish, model it and then have students practice the procedure. The goal is to develop independent learners.

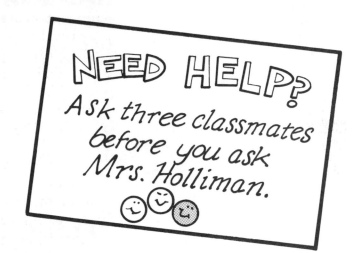

6. Sharing time.

Plan a five- to ten-minute sharing time to bring closure to a busy and active time of the day. Sharing time provides an opportunity for children to share center experiences and products such as an original poem, art project, or the results of a science experiment. Sharing time gives you the opportunity to reinforce the good things that happen during centers, and it provides time for the class to discuss problems and propose solutions.

What about assessment and evaluation?

Using centers actually makes it easier to assess and evaluate individual student progress. Centers free you up and allow you to monitor and interact with children more than you may have in the past. You have more time to make anecdotal records and to conference with students. And because children work independently at centers, you can find out what they can really do on their own.

Anecdotal Records

Centers provide the perfect opportunity to observe students as they work on activities and collaborate with others. Start slowly; write about each student once or twice a month. Trying to write about every student once a week can be overwhelming. You can always increase the number if you find you can handle more.

Using sticky notes is a quick and easy way to organize anecdotal records. Divide a file folder into squares big enough for the sticky notes. Label each square with a child's name, and place a sticky note in the square. Keep the folder with you as you "roam the room" so you can jot down anecdotal records. At the end of each month, place the notes in student portfolios.

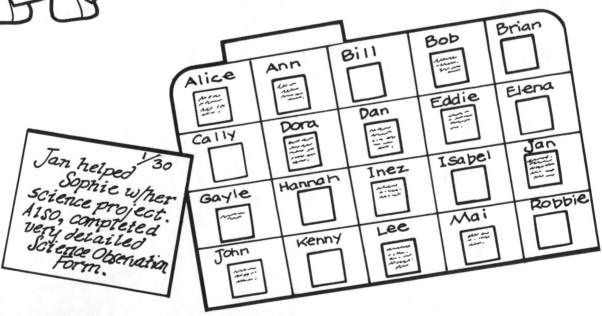

Jan helped Sophie w/her science project. Also, completed very detailed Science Observation form. 1/30

Creative Teaching Press

Conferencing

Using centers allows you more time and flexibility for conferencing with students. As you discuss center projects, you can make anecdotal records, tape the conference, or check off skills that students have mastered. Take the time to ask questions and hear "how" or "why" something was done. Then teacher and student can collaborate on what work should go into the portfolio. Conferencing with students about their accomplishments and setting new goals is an efficient and effective way to use your time and skills as an educator.

Center Boxes and Folders

The center boxes and folders described on page 31 are valuable tools to use in gathering and organizing ongoing and completed center projects. Since each child stores his or her current work in the box or folder, it becomes an instant assessment and evaluation resource. The work can then be discussed at conferences, placed in the child's portfolio, used to determine a grade, or looked over and sent home. Some students will need to have their box or folder monitored on a daily, mid-week, or mid-rotation basis. Most children's folders can be checked at the end of the week or rotation.

Center Journals

At the end of center time each day, students can complete a journal entry describing their center experiences. This journal provides a record of accomplishments and is an excellent resource for assessment and evaluation. Share journals with parents and administrators to show them that centers are a busy and productive part of the day.

oct 6
I went to the Science Center today. Brent and I worked on the elektricity experment. We used wires and a batery to make a cirkit.
Danielle

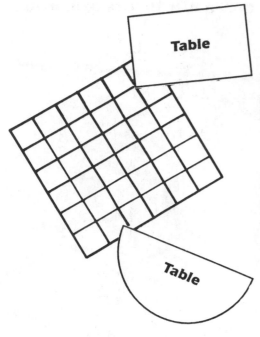

Setting Up the Room

What about my room?

When planning how and where to set up centers, take a close look at your classroom with the following considerations in mind:

- ◆ Create logical traffic patterns so children can move about easily even when all centers are in use.

- ◆ Separate quiet and noisy activities. For example, don't put the Dramatic Play Center right next to the Reading Center.

- ◆ Provide some private spaces for individual work.

- ◆ Provide a large floor space for group collaboration.

- ◆ Create a small area for teacher conferencing and flex-grouping.

- ◆ Use space efficiently. Place the Art and Cooking Centers near a sink and the Computer and Listening Centers near an electrical outlet.

If you are lucky enough to have plenty of space and extra furniture in your classroom, you can set up permanent center locations. These centers can stay in place at all times. Only the activities will change. (Using the Room Arranger reproducible on page 131 to plan your room arrangement will save you lots of time.)

What if my classroom space is limited?

All centers do not need to be separate areas of the classroom. If space and furniture are at a premium, consider the solutions described below.

Desks, Tables, Counters

If your desks are pushed together in small groups, each grouping can become a different center area for your center time. Materials for temporary centers can be stored in labeled boxes, bags, cans, or tubs brought out at center time. You can also divide a large table or counter top into fourths or halves with colored tape. Each section can be used for a different center activity, or each section can be a separate center.

Display Boards

Cardboard display boards make effective movable centers. You can set them up anywhere—on desks, tables, shelves, counters, or even on the floor or in the hallway. Use Velcro to attach activity directions and lightweight materials to the board.

Study Carrels

Study carrels make great centers for one or two children. Look in the library or ask your custodian to check for carrels which might be hidden away in the basement or storage areas.

Corners

Arrange the room so that corners are used in a productive way. An easy chair, pillows, and tubs of books will transform a quiet corner into a cozy Reading Center. A dark corner is the perfect spot for an Overhead Projector Center.

Doors

The closet door, outside door, and cabinet doors are all potential centers. Place materials and supplies in bags or boxes and hang them on hooks. Attach directions, charts, etc. with Velcro so they can be easily changed.

Creative Teaching Press

Bulletin Boards

Using a bulletin board as a center is an efficient use of space. Depending on how large your bulletin board is, you may use it for one center or divide it with yarn to create two or three centers. For example, to create a Research Center, post activity directions and hang lightweight materials such as question cards, informative articles, and photos on the board. Stack research books below the board.

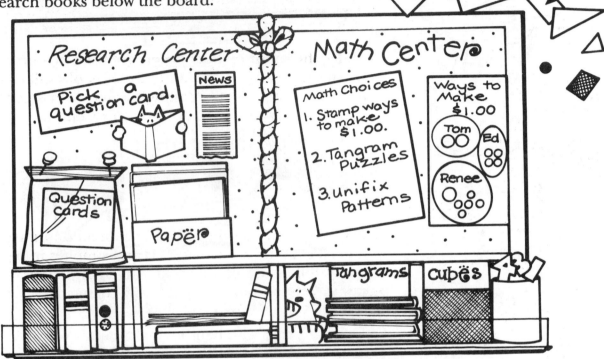

File Cabinets and Magnetic Boards

If you have a file cabinet in your room, you have an instant center. Pull it out of the corner and position it so both sides are accessible. Develop cards for any curriculum area you want to reinforce, stick magnetic tape on the back, and invite children to manipulate the cards on the sides of the cabinet.

Resealable Plastic Bags

Fill one- and two-gallon plastic bags with materials, punch a hole in the top, and hang them from hooks on the wall, under the chalkboard, or on a bulletin board. Children can easily see what's inside. For example, if you fill a bag with several magnets, objects to test, and a workmat for sorting, you have an instant Science Center activity.

Gift Bags

Colorful gift bags with handles make handy portable centers. (You can also use gift bags in permanent centers to store specific activities.) Place all the necessary center activities in the bag, and students can carry it to any part of the room for center time. For example, for a quick Math Center, place money, money stamps, an ink pad, paper, and money story problems in a bag.

You can find decorated bags to represent many different themes such as animals, travel, birthdays, and flowers. A flowered bag can be used for a science activity on identifying the parts of a flower. A museum bag can hold artifacts and books on ancient Egypt.

Creative Teaching Press

Five-Drawer Chest

Consider using an old five-drawer chest to create centers in limited space. Paint the chest white and each drawer a different color. Put activities and materials into each of the drawers. Divide your class into five groups. When it's center time, pull out the drawers and set them around the room. Assign groups to each center by color, rotating each day to a different drawer. Cleanup is quick and easy as materials go back into the drawer. Change the activities in the drawers each week.

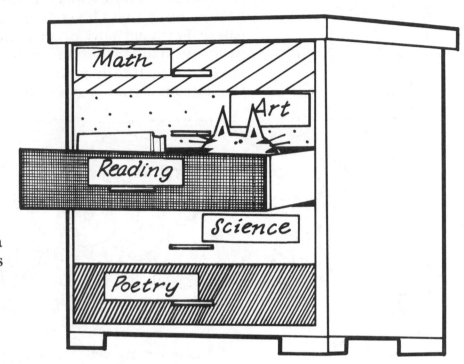

Chains

Large, plastic chains with attached clothespins are useful for organizing materials at a center, and no shelves or tables are needed. (You can find these chains at home improvement stores, baby stores, and hardware stores.) For example, at the Science Center, place a different activity in each bag, hang the bags on the chain, and let students choose which activity they want to do. If space is really at a premium, hang five different bags, one for the Math Center, one for the Listening Center, etc.

Storage Tubs

Use durable, plastic tubs to create portable centers. Label each tub and fill it with one or more activities that students can do at center time. For example, develop a Writing Center in a tub. Include different kinds of paper, writing utensils, clipboards, and writing ideas for students who need suggestions.

Tubs are also a good way to organize materials within a center. For example, put all the equipment and the directions for a science experiment in a tub. Store classroom library books by topic in labeled tubs at the Reading Center.

Lunch Boxes

Old metal and plastic lunch boxes can be found at garage sales and provide a great way to create centers that are "on the go." Spray-paint the metal ones, and cover the picture on the plastic ones with contact paper. Fill them with materials so students can carry the portable mini-centers right to their desks. For example, place rubber stamps, a stamp pad, and adding machine paper in a lunch box. Students can stamp and label patterns as a Math Center activity. To use a lunch box as a mini-Reading Center, place several small books in the box with a tablecloth to spread out for a book picnic.

44

Boxes

Boxes are easy to stack and store for center use. Look in the yellow pages under "Box" to find listings for companies that sell boxes. You may be able to purchase seconds or rejects for very little money. Cover them with contact paper or spray paint. For example, label a box Science Center and include several different activities, each in a separate container.

One-Gallon Cans

Ask cafeteria employees to save one-gallon cans for you. Cut off any rough edges and tape them if necessary. Cover the cans with contact paper or spray paint. Fill each can with materials for one activity—such as measuring cups, measuring spoons, small containers, and beans for an activity on volume and equivalent measures.

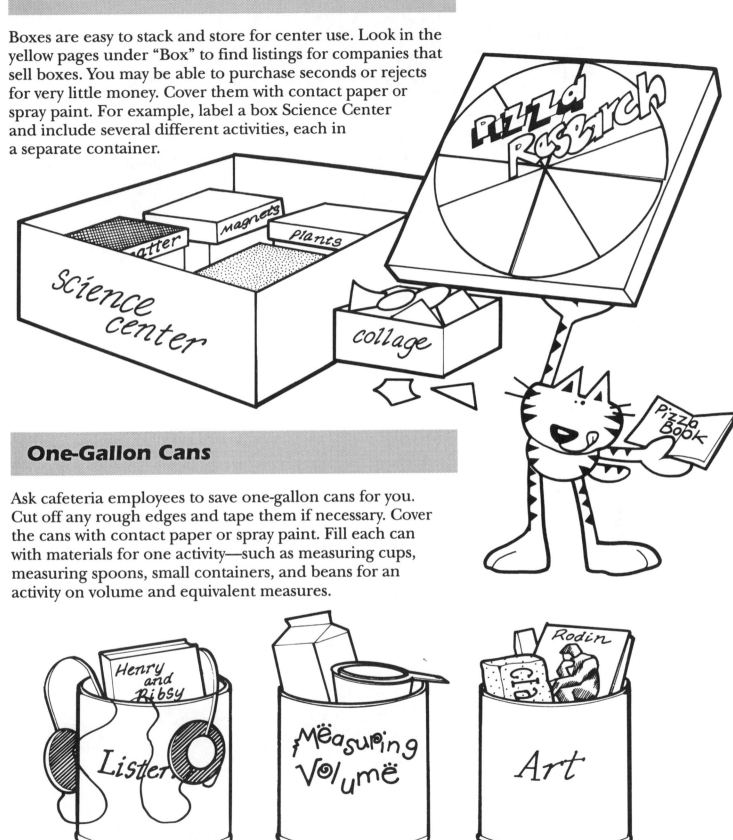

Center
Activities

Writing Center

The Writing Center gives children the opportunity for many different writing experiences. Try to make writing experiences real and purposeful for the individual student. Also include ideas that spark the desire to write.

Materials

- paper: lined, unlined, variety of sizes, colors, shapes
- adding machine tape
- index cards
- scrap paper (Ask your local print shop for scraps.)
- stamps and stamp pads for rebus stories
- alphabet stamps and date stamp
- writing instruments: pens, markers, pencils, colored pencils, crayons, chalk, dry-erase markers
- chalkboards, dry-erase boards, magic slates
- magnetic letters and board
- greeting cards
- stationery and envelopes
- dictionary
- thesaurus
- publishing materials
- blank books
- computer
- typewriter
- magazines
- props
- individual writing and spelling folders
- class dictionary
- alphabet chart
- mailbox

Creative Teaching Press

Writing List

Introduce the Writing Center by having the children tell you all the reasons for writing. Make a list and place it in the center as a reminder. Add to the list as the year progresses.

Paper and Pencils

A fun choice of writing materials encourages kids to write. Ask your local print shop to donate scrap paper (any color or size). Also collect seasonal and thematic pens and pencils.

Writing Folders

Provide a file folder for each child to store their works in progress. The folder can also be used for individualizing spelling. When a child asks how to spell a word, write it on the folder for future reference.

Writing Topics

Encourage children to keep an ongoing list of things they want to write about. Use story starters only if students can't think of a writing topic.

Writing Center Quick Tips

Community Writing

Cover a table with white butcher paper for "Community Writing." You can divide the paper into individual spaces, or allow a free flow. Beginning writers love this activity.

Editors and Writers

Invite older students to be guest editors. Let them help out at the Writing Center. Young children will love the attention and support.

Dry-Erase Boards

Individual dry-erase boards are a favorite with children of all ages. Children can write, revise, and edit with ease. When they have finished, you can copy their text on the copy machine, and they will be ready to illustrate and publish!

Adding Machine Tape

Adding machine tape is perfect for writing tall tale stories. Hang it up with string at the Writing Center and let kids roll off what they need. It's also great for making any kind of list.

Writing Center Activities

Theme Words

Calendar cutouts are inexpensive and handy for developing word banks to fit a season or theme. For example, using pumpkin cutouts, brainstorm a list of "pumpkin" or fall words with the class. Write one word on each pumpkin. Post the cutouts on a chart or bulletin board. Students can use the words to spark ideas and to check spelling when writing stories.

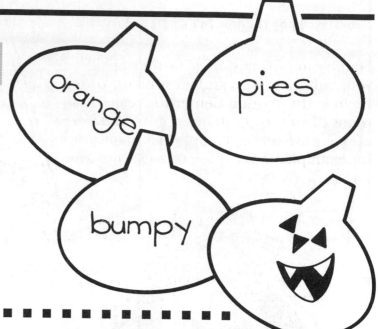

Letter Writing

Letter writing is a life skill, and it's fun, especially if you get an answer. *Messages in the Mailbox* by Loreen Leedy is a good book to use to introduce different types of letter writing. Stock the center with a wide variety of stationery, envelopes, and postcards, and give students the opportunity to write letters on a weekly basis. Some authentic letter-writing opportunities are:

- friendly letters to classmates, family, principal, support staff
- get-well cards, birthday cards, holiday cards
- invitations to class presentations
- letters of inquiry (When will NASA launch the next Space Shuttle?)
- letters to the editor
- letters to a favorite author, celebrity, government leader
- letters to cross-age buddies
- letters to seniors in a convalescent home

Creative Teaching Press

Rebus Stories

Stamp out boring stories! Gather up all your rubber stamps and let students use them at the Writing Center to create rebus stories. You can often purchase inexpensive sets of stamps on a theme, for example, outer space or zoo animals.

Props

Create a writing prop box. Children love playing the part of the character they are writing about. Provide hats and costumes to help with the creativity. A pirate hat, eye patch, and sash will inspire students to create exciting "Ahoy Matey" pirate adventures or a descriptive written portrait of a pirate.

Writing to a Class Pet

Young students love to write letters to a class pet. Make a special little mailbox just for Rascal the Rat or Harvey the Hamster, and watch the mail pour in. You might want to have a designated time for kids to read their letters out loud to the pet or get an older student to respond to the letters.

Notepad Notables

There are so many fabulous notepads available in all shapes and sizes. Use these to suggest writing activities for students like the ones shown. Have kids respond to the notepad prompts by writing on a blank notepad sheet of the same design.

Things a frog would say

mush LOVE Cupid hug heart

Describe something you can make from apples

Greeting Card Starters

Look for greeting cards that have interesting pictures on the front. Show the card to the children. Ask them to brainstorm words they might need if they were going to write about the picture on the card. List their words on the inside of the card. Keep the cards in a box at the Writing Center. This is also a good way to recycle used greeting cards.

hibernate Grizzly fur, cave cubs huge paws

Bag a Story

Place seven objects in a lunch bag. Have students fold a piece of paper into eight sections. Ask them to introduce a character in the first section and write a story using all of the objects in the bag as part of the story, one section for each object.

| This is about a dog named Mopsy. | Moosy liked to chase baseballs. | When burglars came to steal the silver forks | She couldn't bark, so... She made balloon noises. |
| Her owners were so happy they colored her dog house with red markers. | They fed her dog bones whenever she wanted them. | They wouldn't let her drink from a cup so... | they taught her to drink from a straw! slurp! |

52

Work in Progress

A published work isn't necessarily "perfect." Remember, your authors are in the process.

Books! Books! Books!

Teach your children how to make a variety of books such as, Flip-Flap Books, Pop-up Books, Person Books, and Paper Bag Books. (See pages 132–135 for bookmaking directions.)

Publishing Musts

- yarn
- stapler
- ribbon
- lunch bags
- binder rings
- rubber bands
- paper plates
- poster board
- newspapers
- paper fasteners
- butcher paper
- colored masking tape
- wrapping paper
- markers
- crayons
- brads
- hole punch

Professional Publishers

To give books a professional look, add some of the following elements: title page, publishing information, dedication page, short biography of the author, a book jacket.

■ ■ ■ ■ ■ ■ ■ ■ ■ ■
Publishing Quick Tips
■ ■ ■ ■ ■ ■ ■ ■ ■ ■

Readers' Comments

Glue an envelope onto the final blank page of the book. Place a Readers' Comment sheet in the envelope. Friends, neighbors, relatives, and classmates can write comments about the book. What a motivation for young authors!

Recycle and Write

Make Poof Books (instructions on page 134) out of newspapers, paper grocery bags, and used wrapping paper. They're cheap and kids can even make them at home.

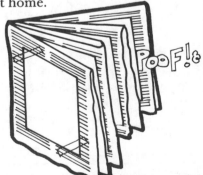

Be Prepared

Schedule a volunteer one day a week to help with publishing. Volunteers can make book covers, help with editing, or assemble books.

Make It Fun

When asked what she liked best about first grade, Maggie replied, "Publishing!" Make that a goal for your students.

Listening Center

Students have lots of opportunities throughout the school day to listen in a large group setting, but the Listening Center offers them opportunities for independent listening activities.

Materials

- blank tapes
- books and tapes
- class-made books and tapes
- tape recorder
- individual tape players
- headphones
- resealable plastic bags
- song and poem charts

Get Organized

Store books and tapes in resealable plastic bags or in a hanging shoe bag. Large, cafeteria-size tin cans are also good. Put a book and a matching tape in the can, and hook the headphones over the side.

On the Move

Put a tape player, some headphones, and tapes in a tub. Let kids take this portable center anywhere there is a free electrical plug.

Record a Story

The Listening Center is for listening and recording. Encourage children to record an original story or book with sound effects.

Cool Listening

Individualize with Walkman tape players. Several children can be in the Listening Center making individual choices.

Listening Center Quick Tips

Instant Taping Session

Save time by taping as you read a book to the whole class. Leave the tape on as you discuss the story. Kids love hearing themselves and their classmates.

Red Light, Green Light

Be sure to use color coding to indicate buttons on the tape recorder. Green means play, red means stop, yellow means rewind.

Nature and More

Tapes can reflect a child's world and introduce them to a new one! Tape nature, household, and animal sounds. (Look for commercially produced sound tapes.)

Voice Variations

Put variety in homemade tapes by having parent volunteers tape-record books. Teach them to use "voices" and read with enthusiasm. Don't forget to invite the principal to read too.

Listening Center Activities

My Very Own Tape

Ask each child to bring a blank tape for the Listening Center. Label it with his or her name. Throughout the year, students can record themselves reading original stories, reciting a poem, singing a song, etc. Save the tape and use it for evaluation, play it at parent conferences, or send it home as an end-of- the-year memento.

Tape Talks

Have blank tapes available so that kids can tape get-well messages to a sick classmate, thank-yous to a volunteer, good wishes to a birthday child, compliments to the "person of the week," or news for the principal.

What's That Sound?

Tape-record common sounds around the house: a door closing, ball bouncing, dog barking, car starting, etc. Cut pictures from magazines that correspond to the sounds on the tape. Students can listen and find the matching pictures.

Radio Shows

Older children can create and record a radio show complete with music, stories, commercials, and sound effects at the Listening Center. Readers Theatre scripts work well, or students can create their own radio dramas.

Biographies

Tape short biographical information about famous people. Let students listen to the tape and practice note-taking skills. The information can be summarized on the Person Book on page 135. For younger children, have the Gingerbread Boy, Humpty Dumpty, or other famous characters tell about themselves. Children can listen and then retell, draw, or write notes about what they hear.

Taped Interviews

Have students develop interview questions and tape-record the interviews. They can interview friends, family members, school staff, community leaders, etc. Store the interview tapes at the Listening Center and feature one interview a week.

Reading Center

The Reading Center should be a comfortable place where students can relax and enjoy a good book. It's also a place where students can interact with each other as they read with a partner or discuss books they've read.

Materials

- books from all genres
- bookmarks
- big books
- student-made books
- pillows, beanbag chair, rocker
- Reading-the-Room pointers
- Special Specs (See page 63.)
- pocket charts and sentence strips
- theme-related books
- magazines and newspapers
- flannel board and props
- bookcases
- lamp
- small tent, wading pool
- artificial tree

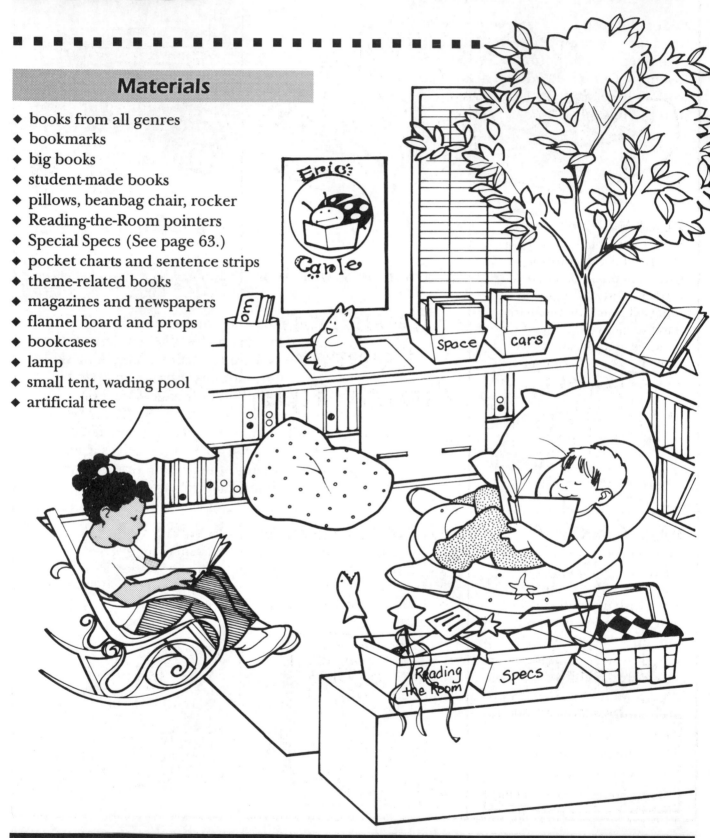

Creative Teaching Press

Read, Read, Read

Children become better readers by reading. Give them uninterrupted time to do it.

The Reading Teacher

You are an important model. Kids need to see you reading every day.

Tub It

Organize books in tubs thematically. They are easy to find and easy to store. Introduce new theme book tubs throughout the year.

I Lost My Place

Write each child's name on a 4" x 12" sheet of construction paper. Laminate these book markers, and store them in a can. Children slide the marker into the spot where they removed a book from a tub or shelf.

Reading Center Quick Tips

Tree-mendous Reading

Make the Reading Center an inviting place. An artificial tree with tiny white lights will make it magic!

Book Bonanza

Display the best books being offered in your book club order. Do a little commercial about each one and see how your book orders grow.

Bonus Points = More Books
More Books = More Variety
More Variety = More Choices
More Choices = More Reading

My Very Favorite Book

Each week display "My Very Favorite Book" in the reading center. Kids can't keep their hands off the teacher's favorite.

Read All About It

Current events become a natural discussion topic when newspapers are in the Reading Center.

Celebrate Reading

Make every month National Read-a-Book Month. Declare September "Animal-Story Month." October can be "Scary-Book Month," etc.

Log It

Provide a reading log for each child to keep track of the books they have read.

Camp Read-a-Lot

Pitch a small tent for a reading getaway. Make a "campfire" by gluing rocks on a pizza board and adding wood.

Subscribe Today

Magazines are a must! Look for small magazine racks at garage sales, and ask the class to bring in used magazines of interest to students.

More Reading Center Quick Tips

Make Yourself at Home

Make the Reading Center comfortable. Add big pillows, a lamp, and a rocking chair.

Student Authors

Don't forget to include students' published books and class books in the Reading Center. These original works are usually their very favorite books!

Make a Splash

Blow up a small wading pool and watch kids dive into reading. Add pillows for reading comfort.

Reflections

A reading journal will help children reflect on the book they are reading. Keep journals in a box at the Reading Center so they won't be misplaced.

Creative Teaching Press

Stand Up and Stand Out

Use mini-easels from an office supply store or cookbook holders to feature outstanding books.

Where's Spot?

Use colored self-stick labels to organize your books thematically and seasonally. Some books will need more than one color.

Crawl In and Read

Create a reading cave out of an appliance box. Students can paint the inside and outside of the box. Cut a hole in the top to let light in.

Big Books

An old drying rack is a unique way to hang big books, both commercial and student-made.

■ ■ ■ ■ ■ ■ ■ ■ ■ ■ ■
Even More Reading Center Quick Tips
■ ■ ■ ■ ■ ■ ■ ■ ■ ■

Hang onto Every Word

Tie yarn through the center of paperback books and hang them up for a quick bulletin board display.

It's a Book Picnic

Place picnic baskets full of books in the Reading Center. Include tablecloths to spread out.

Read to Me

Invite a parent or older child to come to the Reading Center at certain times of the day to read aloud to students.

I Can Read!

Your youngest readers can read all kinds of environmental print. Make a scrapbook for the Reading Center.

What Is It?

Reading the Room is a great activity for beginning readers. Students walk around and read the lists, stories, poetry, charts, signs, etc. that are posted around the room.

Just a Few

Limit "Room Readers" to two or three children at a time. Children read to themselves, not to the whole class.

Here's the Point

Children use all kinds of pointers to read the print around the room. Store the pointers in a box in the Reading Center.

Yum! Yum!

Puppets on a stick become "word munchers." Kids will eat up this activity.

Reading the Room

Words That Shine

Using a flashlight as a pointer will make your readers shine!

Splat!

Flyswatters are great pointers, especially for an insect theme. Cut out the center so children can frame the words.

Star Reader

Use a star wand to Read the Room. Make reading magic.

Blooming Readers

Look for silk or plastic flowers with long, thick stems. Watch young readers bloom with this pointer.

Creative Teaching Press

Got an Itch

Back-scratchers are fun Read-the-Room pointers. Your students will say, "I'm itching to read the room."

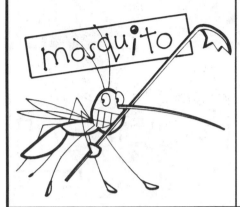

Flip for Reading

A spatula will make a great wide pointer.

Pencil Pointers

Unsharpened pencils with thematic and seasonal toppers are great short pointers.

Brush Up on Reading

February is Dental Health Month. Use a jumbo toothbrush as a pointer.

■ ■ ■ ■ ■ ■ ■ ■ ■

More Reading the Room

■ ■ ■ ■ ■ ■ ■ ■ ■

Collect Specs

Collect old glasses from everyone. Take out the lenses and you have great specs for Reading the Room.

Special Specs

Make reading spec-tacular! Inexpensive theme and seasonal glasses are out there. Look for them and add to your collection. Check party shops.

Create-a-Spec

Children can design their own special specs using the pattern on page 136.

Big Words

Jumbo specs are essential for reading BIG WORDS.

Poetry Center

Poetry nurtures a love of language and invites children to see, hear, and feel in new ways. Building on a child's natural love of rhythm and rhyme, the Poetry Center gives children the opportunity to read, create, and share poems.

Materials

- poetry anthologies and collections
- poetry books by individual authors
- poems in "book form" (*Hiawatha, Casey at the Bat, The Owl and the Pussycat, etc.*)
- poetry posters
- nursery rhymes
- pocket charts with poetry on sentence strips
- pencils, pens, markers
- paper, variety of sizes and colors
- chalkboard and chalk
- individual-size dry-erase boards
- dry-erase pens
- models of various kinds of poetry
- rhyming dictionary
- tape recorder

Creative Teaching Press

Poetry Time

Begin and end the day with a nursery rhyme or poem, or take a surprise poetry break during class. The teacher can lead the poetry break, or the kids can sign up and take turns.

Poem of the Week

Display a favorite poem each week on a poster, on a bulletin board, or in a pocket chart. Read the poem each day. Invite students to memorize it and recite it for the class. Encourage them to write poems on a similar theme.

Poetry Forms

Make a list and post samples of different kinds of poetry appropriate for your students, such as haiku, limericks, cinquains, couplets, and free verse.

Poetry on Tape

Provide a tape player and headphones so children can listen to the sounds of poetry. You or your students can record favorite or original poems, or you can use commercial poetry tapes.

Poetry Center Quick Tips

Magic Words

Provide a set of teacher-made or purchased magnetic words. Students can manipulate the words to create free-verse poems on a magnetic board or the side of a file cabinet.

Break Out into Poetry

Kids love hearing their teacher "break out into poetry." Commit a few poems to memory. It will inspire the kids and will come in handy during your golden years.

Shape Notepads

Have a variety of shape notepads available for children to write their poetry on. Commercially made notepads are inexpensive and come in a great variety of shapes.

National Poetry Month

April is National Poetry Month. Celebrate with a poetry party. Invite parents or another class for a poetry reading session (originals or old favorites). Don't forget the refreshments.

Poetry Center Activities

Pocket Chart Poetry

For young children, write familiar nursery rhymes on sentence strips. Make a picture card for each strip. Students can match the pictures to each line as they chant the rhyme. Familiar songs—poems set to music—work well for this activity too.

Children can also use rhyming picture cards to create their own poems in a pocket chart. Place an unfinished couplet in the pocket chart. Have students complete the couplet with rhyming picture cards. As children have more experience, change the poetry frame and add additional lines.

Jump-Rope Rhymes

Jump-rope rhymes are "poetry in motion." Gather books on jump-rope rhymes, such as *Anna Banana: 101 Jump-Rope Rhymes* by Joanna Cole and Stephanie Calmenson. Place some jump ropes at the Poetry Center, and let students jump as they recite their favorite rhymes. You may want to let students jump outside or in a hallway. Encourage them to make up jump-rope rhymes and teach them to the class.

Creative Teaching Press

Rhyming Word File

Create a box of rhyming words. Brainstorm rhyming words with students and list the words on cards. Continue adding to each list as students discover more rhyming words in the poems they read and write.

Rhyming Lotto

For younger students make various lotto boards with rhyming picture cards. Store each set (board and matching cards) in separate resealable bags. Students match the rhyming picture cards to the lotto board. Later they can make a rhyming Flip-Flap Book using some of the illustrations from the lotto game. (See page 132 for directions on making the Flip-Flap Book.)

Birthday Poems

To celebrate student birthdays, have each child write a short poem about the birthday boy or girl. Use the frame shown, or have students create their own. Post the poems on a birthday bulletin board, or place them in a gift bag. What a great present from the whole class!

Mini-Poetry Book

Share a variety of poems that have been published in book form such as *Casey at the Bat* by Ernest Thayer, *The Owl and the Pussycat* by Edward Lear, *The Night Before Christmas* by Clement C. Moore, or *The Magic Wood* by Henry Treece. Have students make a poetry book. First they chose a favorite short poem. Ask them to copy and illustrate one stanza on each page of the book. Or have students work in small groups for this activity.

Poetry Place Mats

Each month or season have children make poetry place mats for their families. They can copy favorite poems from anthologies or write their own in the center of the paper and add illustrations and border designs. What a great mealtime menu—haiku and hamburgers!

Rhyming Dictionary

Place a commercial rhyming dictionary at the center. Have children choose an ending sound, find the sound in the dictionary, and write an original poem using as many rhyming words as possible. Provide models of poems with different patterns. Try different rhyming patterns such as AA, ABCB, or ABAB.

Poetry Plates

Pick a theme. It could be the current season or a topic the class is studying. Ask each student to write a couplet in the center of a paper plate. The couplet should fit the theme the class has selected. After the plates are decorated, assemble them into a class book and add the book to the Poetry Center. Vary the activity by inviting students to write two lines of free verse instead of couplets.

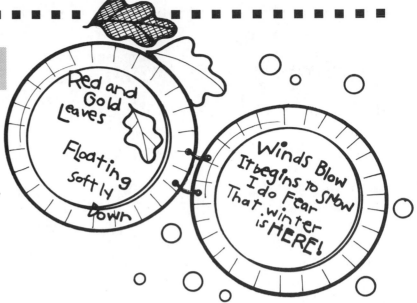

Stitch a Poem

Samplers were popular in the 1700s and 1800s. Ask older students to write a couplet, print it with pencil on any solid-color heavy fabric, and stitch over the words with heavy embroidery thread. When finished, mat their handiwork and send it home ready to frame. (Remember to make the poetry sampler a standard frame size.) As an alternative, students could use embroidery paint.

List Poem

A list poem is an easy format for beginning poetry writing experiences. Students pick a topic and brainstorm words related to the topic. The next step is to assemble the words into a list that is pleasing to the ear. It's fun to write these poems on long narrow strips of paper. For very young students, write the words on cards and let them use the cards to compose their poem. They can assemble the cards to create different versions of the poem and then choose their favorite.

Math Center

It's as easy as 1, 2, 3 to get kids involved in numbers, measuring, and problem solving when you stock your Math Center with hands-on materials. Children can explore math concepts, practice new skills, and apply skills they have mastered.

Materials

- collectible manipulatives: buttons, keys, colored pasta, golf tees, toothpicks, colored paper clips, beans
- plastic counters, all shapes and colors
- pattern blocks
- Base Ten Blocks
- Cuisenaire® Rods
- attribute blocks
- tangrams
- graph paper
- math-related literature
- balance scales
- measuring instruments (rulers, yardsticks, cups, measuring spoons)
- geoboards
- fraction models
- play money
- clock
- timer
- calculators
- games and puzzles
- dice and spinners
- floor graph
- magnetic board
- magnetic shapes and numbers

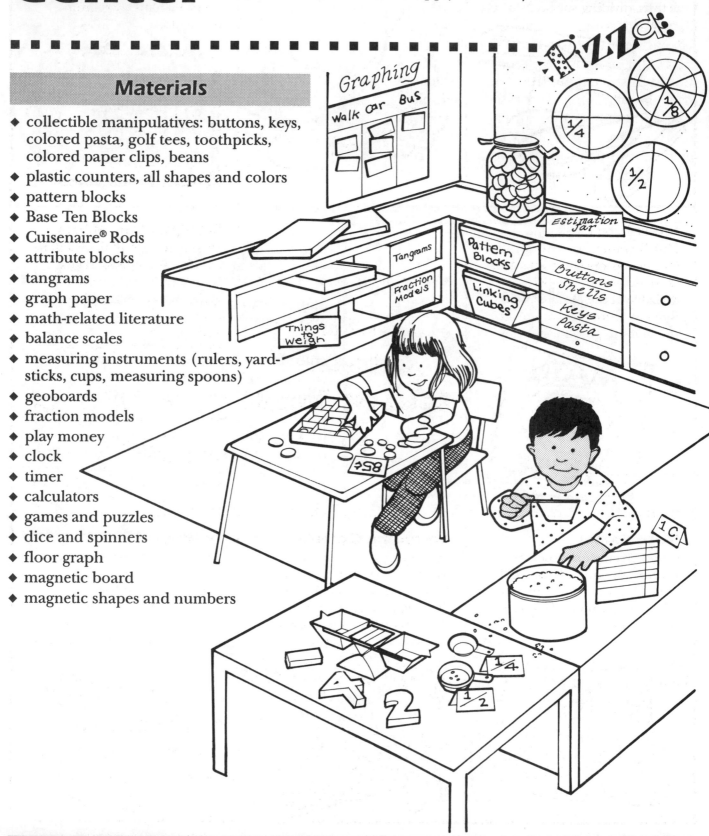

Real World

Make math meaningful. Show kids how it applies to the real world: making change at the store, measuring for a cooking activity, dividing snacks into equal shares.

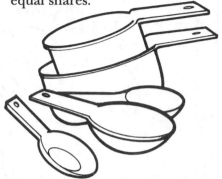

Making Manipulatives

Make theme-related manipulatives out of Fimo modeling material, or let students make their own. They love it!

Work Mats

When appropriate, provide individual math work mats. A designated working space helps kids organize their work and keeps manipulatives from getting lost.

Literature Link

Link literature to math by having appropriate books, such as *Math Curse* by Jon Scieszka, available at the Math Center. Kids can write their own word problems to go with the story.

Math Center Quick Tips

Manipulative Mania

Search out manipulatives that are fun and unusual. Look at craft stores for seasonal garlands to cut up and use as counters for any math operation. For place value, cut the garlands into tens and ones.

Math Games

Commercial games such as Yahtzee, dominos, chess, and bingo develop math and logic skills. Place games like these at the Math Center.

Recording Options

Provide a variety of ways for students to record what they have done in the math center: drawings, rubber stamps, stickers, real objects, math journals, charts, graphs.

Do It Again

Have students use a variety of manipulatives to work on the same skill or concept. For example, use Base Ten Blocks, plastic linking cubes, and beansticks for place-value work.

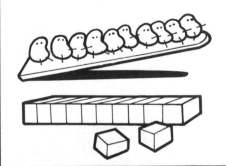

Math Center Activities

Writing Numerals

For young children who are just learning to write numerals, provide lots of "touchable" models that students can trace over with their fingers. You can cut numerals out of sandpaper, corrugated cardboard, fuzzy fabric, and embossed papers. Or you can glue cotton balls, rice, pasta, beans, sand, or yarn on pieces of tagboard to form numerals. Children love to use these tactile numerals with a blindfold for a guessing game.

Students can practice forming numerals in many ways without using paper and pencil. They can write in small sand trays or on magic slates. They can form numerals with yarn, string, playdough, modeling clay, buttons, or toothpicks. They can make rubber band numerals on geoboards. They can even make edible numerals with refrigerator biscuit dough.

72

Estimation Station

Feature independent estimation activities at your Math Center. One of the easiest is the Estimation Jar. Each week, fill it with different objects. Use large objects such as walnuts or marshmallows for younger children. For older children use smaller objects such as marbles, pennies, or goldfish crackers. Let each child examine the jar and write their estimate on a slip of paper. At the end of the week, count the objects together.

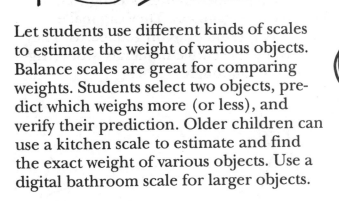

Students can estimate the capacity of a variety of containers. Provide standard or nonstandard measuring scoops and cups plus a pourable solid such as rice or beans. Students estimate how many scoops will fill the container and then test their prediction. Ask them to fill the container half way and see if they want to revise the estimate before filling it to the top. Use a drop cloth or tray for easy cleanup.

Let students use different kinds of scales to estimate the weight of various objects. Balance scales are great for comparing weights. Students select two objects, predict which weighs more (or less), and verify their prediction. Older children can use a kitchen scale to estimate and find the exact weight of various objects. Use a digital bathroom scale for larger objects.

Money

The Math Center is the perfect place for children to practice and apply money skills. Using real coins at the center will ensure greater transfer to real-life experiences with money. Young children can identify, sort, and graph coins. They can use nickels to count by fives and dimes to count by tens.

5, 10, 15, 20...

A set of money stamps is great for recording work. Students can record answers to money problems, create rebus story problems involving money, and stamp out different money combinations for a given amount. For example, there are 293 ways to change a dollar bill. Provide a large piece of butcher paper and the money stamps. As an ongoing center activity, let students stamp out the different combinations. Younger children can stamp different ways to make ten cents or twenty-five cents.

Set up a mini-toy store or grocery store. Mark prices on all the items. Encourage students to role-play shoppers and the cashier, paying for purchases and making change. Or stock the center with take-out restaurant menus. Students can "order" off a menu, staying within a designated budget for one, two, or three dinners.

$1.49

$2.38

98¢

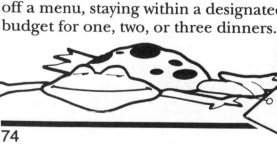

69¢

Graphing

As students learn how to make and read graphs, they must gather, organize, record, and analyze sets of data. These are important problem-solving skills. For concrete graphing experiences, provide collections of objects that students can sort and graph. Ask questions to stimulate investigations. Small objects, such as seeds or shells, can be sorted into empty egg cartons or ice-cube trays to make instant graphs. For graphing larger objects, provide a floor graph. Students can sort and graph collections of socks, mittens, crayons, small toy animals, food boxes, cans of food, books, etc.

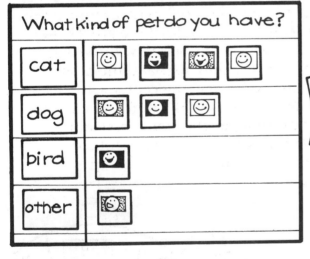

Provide different ways for students to record graphing information. They can draw original pictures, use rubber stamps, stickers, or cutouts and create bar or line graphs on graphing paper. Older students can pick their own graphing topics and survey class members to make graphs.

You can encourage students to make a daily visit to the Math Center by posting a question of the day in a pocket chart. Prepare a photo card or a name card for each student that can be reused. Children answer the question and place their photo card in the appropriate pocket chart row to form a graph. For older children, use a Venn diagram format and sticky notes for students' names.

Fractions

Stock the center with manipulatives so students can explore fractions as equal parts of a whole and as equal parts of a set. In addition to commercial products such as color tiles, pattern blocks, Cuisenaire® Rods, fraction bars, and plastic linking cubes, common classroom materials can also be used. Provide paper shapes and graph paper to fold and cut. Students can also use toothpicks, buttons, coins, or plastic counters for finding equal parts of a set.

Bring out a tub of rice and let students fill containers ½, ¼, or ⅓ full. Students can also use standard measuring cups and spoons to discover equivalent measures. (e.g., How many teaspoons make a table-spoon? What fraction is that?)

Don't forget to include books about fractions that kids can read and share with each other. A few titles are: *Eating Fractions* by Bruce McMillan, *Gator Pie* by Louise Mathews, and *Fraction Action* by Loreen Leedy.

76

Math Notables

Shape notepads are versatile materials for creating fun Math Center activities. Look for notepads that suggest an accompanying manipulative; for example a frog notepad with plastic flies or a leaf notepad with nuts in the shell. Any notepad can be used for counting, computation, story problems, or place value. Be creative; there are lots of possibilities.

Math Stamps

Kids will stampede the Math Center when you use rubber stamps. Start collecting stamps now: pictures, coins, numerals, designs. They can record math problems such as those shown below.

To illustrate addition and subtraction:

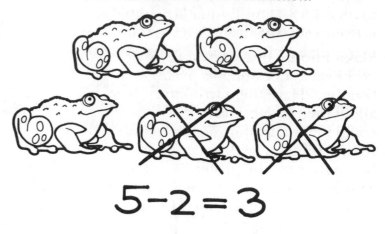

$$5 - 2 = 3$$

To record multiplication facts:

$$2 \times 3 = 6$$

To make and extend patterns:

To count by twos, fives, and tens:

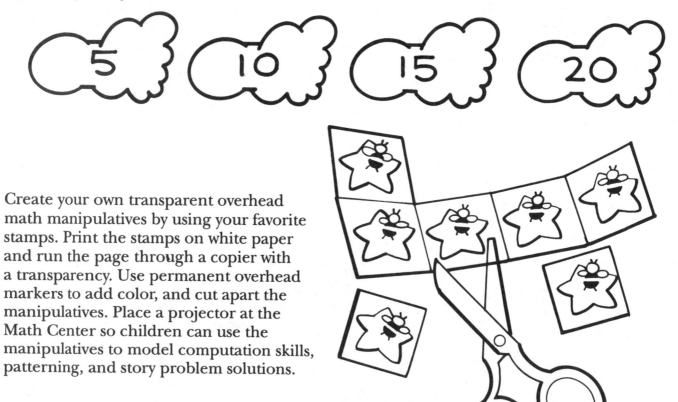

Create your own transparent overhead math manipulatives by using your favorite stamps. Print the stamps on white paper and run the page through a copier with a transparency. Use permanent overhead markers to add color, and cut apart the manipulatives. Place a projector at the Math Center so children can use the manipulatives to model computation skills, patterning, and story problem solutions.

Creative Teaching Press

Math in a Bag

Lunch bags aren't just for lunches. Use them for a variety of fun Math Center activities such as those described below.

Make a house by cutting a point at the top of the sack. Let students decorate their "houses." Have them write story problems about their family and house. The story could include family members, pets, bedrooms, number of doors and windows, etc. Students store the problems in the house. This becomes an instant math activity as students try to solve each others' problems.

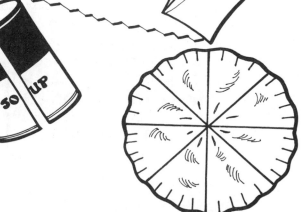

Use bags for a variety of estimation activities. Students can estimate how many objects are in a bag, how much the bag weighs, how many rocks a bag will hold before it breaks, the area or perimeter of the bag, how many Styrofoam pieces it will hold, and the circumference of an inflated bag.

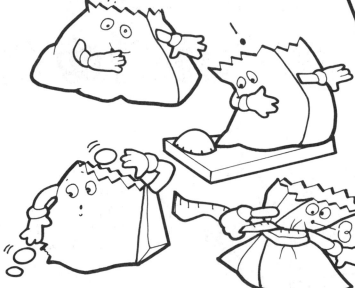

Try some grocery bag math. Place some food pictures in the bag that have been cut into fractional pieces. Students spill out the pieces, match them up, and decide what fractional part each one is. Then have them color and cut out some fraction foods of their own.

Art Center

As you teach kids about color, texture, and line, the Art Center allows them to experiment with concepts they have learned. Provide specific activities, but don't forget to let students explore the materials and use their own creative ideas.

Materials

- paint (watercolor, tempera, finger paint)
- brushes (various sizes)
- markers, chalk, crayons, colored pencils
- scissors
- sponges, craft sticks, straws
- tape, glue, paste
- collage materials
- art prints
- paper (all kinds and colors)
- fabric
- wallpaper samples
- clay
- stamps and stamp pads
- yarn, string, ribbon
- books on artists
- newspapers

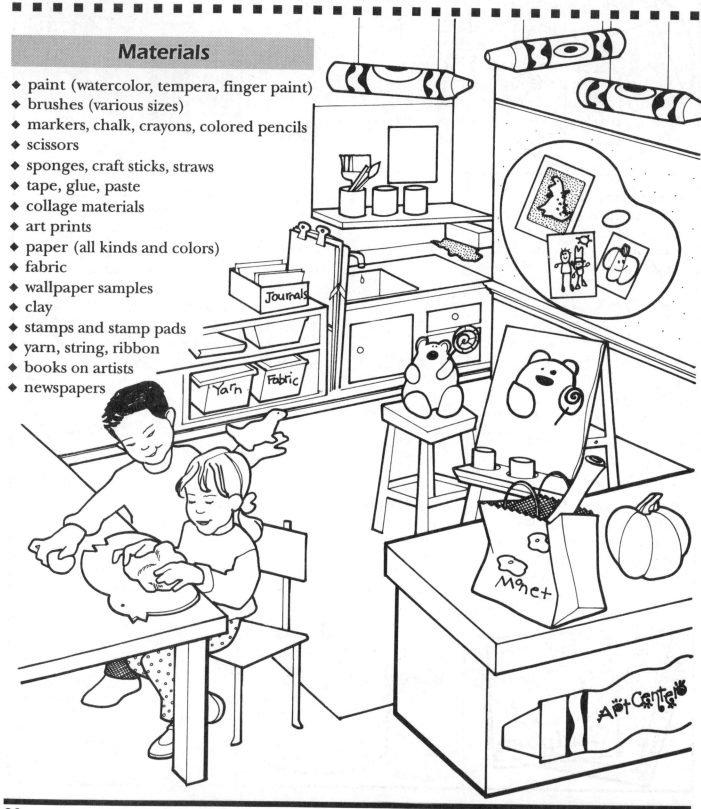

Class Art Gallery

Create an art gallery where student art projects can be displayed. It's an instant ongoing bulletin board!

No More Paint Stains

Add liquid dish soap to tempera paint so it will easily wash out of students' clothes. Parents will thank you.

Vary the Media

Display works by various artists in the center. Label the different art media used.

Ecological Art

Teach kids to conserve paper by using scraps from the scrap box when they only need a small piece of paper.

Art Center Quick Tips

Quick Clay Cleanup

When doing clay projects, have students work on plastic place mats for an easy cleanup.

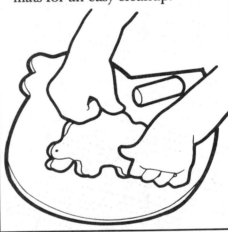

Art Resource Books

Collect art resource books so students can get ideas for new art projects such as collage, puppets, stitchery, clay, etc.

Playdough

Ask for volunteers to make new playdough each month using the recipe on page 137. To give the playdough an inviting smell, add fragrances appropriate to the color of the dough.

Meltdown

Recycle old crayons to make large new ones. Peel paper off crayons and place them in 5-oz paper cups. Microwave at 30-second intervals until melted. When hardened, peel off the cups.

Art Center Activities

Art Journal

Have each child keep an art journal in the form of a sketchbook, and provide lots of opportunities to draw. Not only does this show their artistic progress, but it also becomes a "drawing bank" they can refer to when illustrating their published works.

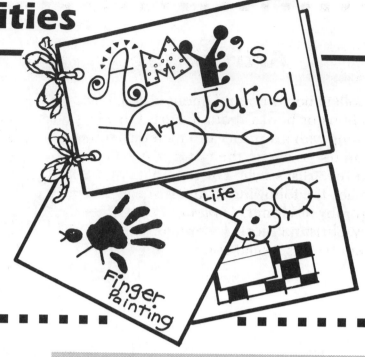

Teach Kids to Draw

Some kids do not feel comfortable with their drawing ability, yet we are constantly asking them to illustrate school projects. Ed Emberley has written a whole series of books taking kids through the process of drawing familiar and seasonal objects as well as animals and people. Collect his books (or similar books) and keep them at the Art Center all year long. Provide plenty of time for students to practice drawing just for the fun of it!

Art Nine Times

Make a grid of nine art projects you want each child to experience over a nine-week period. Put this in their center folder, and ask them to color in each square as they do the project. Leave the materials for each project at the center.

Creative Teaching Press

Artist Bags

Collect books about famous artists. Place a book or books about the artist in a bag along with art prints and materials students can use to create their own masterpiece in the artist's style. For example, for Monet place the following in an artist bag: a biography of Monet, *Linnea in Monet's Garden* by Christina Bjork, watercolor paper, and watercolors. Voila! You're ready to go!

Still Life of the Month

Each month set up a different still life in the Art Center. (You'll enjoy having something still in the room.) Use a variety of objects that children will connect with. You might create a fall scene with pumpkins, leaves, corn, and nuts. A December still life could be an assortment of toys. Be creative and let the children bring objects and help with the display. They'll enjoy drawing or painting the still life.

Social Studies Center

Do you want your students to explore foreign lands, visit the past, or make friends with other cultures? A Social Studies Center can open up a child's world in so many ways. Center activities are well suited for integrating a wide variety of skills.

Materials

- globe
- atlas
- maps (world, country, city)
- compass
- books (fiction, nonfiction, biographies)
- filmstrip projector and filmstrips
- paper
- grocery bags
- camera and film
- tape player
- calendar pictures
- magazines
- newspapers
- encyclopedia
- modeling clay

Room 9's Talking Wall

a local historian came to our class

we learned about Kwanzaa

AFRICA

Creative Teaching Press

On the Go!

Collect postcards, maps, brochures, alphabet books, and pamphlets from other states or countries. Keep them in an old suitcase. Invite students to take a trip using resources at the center.

Candid Camera

Keep a camera loaded and ready to photograph your students in action. Compile these photos into a photographic history of your school year.

Famous People

Keep an area of this center stocked with biographies— pirates, explorers, presidents, cowboys, famous women, scientists. Have students use the Person Book on page 135 to write and illustrate facts they learn.

Career Hats

Have a hat box that contains hats that represent different careers. Kids choose a hat, research the career, and share it with the rest of the class; wearing the hat, of course.

■ ■ ■ ■ ■ ■ ■ ■ ■ ■
Social Studies Center Quick Tips
■ ■ ■ ■ ■ ■ ■ ■ ■ ■

It's About Time

Adding machine tape is perfect for historical time lines. Accordion-fold the tape into sections, add the date, then write and/or illustrate events over time.

Museum Must

Contact your local history museums and see if they have traveling kits or exhibits that you can check out to use in the center.

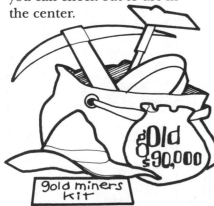

It's in the News

Keep current newspapers and magazines at the center. Kids can clip and classify local, state, national, and international news. Young students can clip pictures of famous people and events in the news.

Picture History

Photographs can speak a thousand words about the past. Collect books, postcards, and posters that show the past through pictures. Garage sales are a good source.

Social Studies Activities

Geography

Provide a 12" x 12" piece of cardboard and a variety of colors of modeling clay. Display a list of geography terms (mesa, river, stream, coast, plains) and have students use modeling clay to create a scene that includes all of the words listed. Have paper and straight pins available so students can label the geographic forms.

Our Neighborhood

Have each child create their house out of a lunch bag. They can also make other neighborhood buildings out of bags: stores, businesses, libraries, etc. When the buildings are completed, put your neighborhood together and map it on the floor. Put something inside the bags so the buildings won't fall over.

Famous Dates

Collect books, such as those listed below, that tell about important events on each day of the year. Invite students to turn to a date and read about the event described on that date. Ask them to share their findings with the class.

- *Do You Know What Day Tomorrow Is?* by Lee Bennett Hopkins and Misha Arenstein
- *Doing the Days* by Lorraine Dahlstrom
- *Chase's Annual Events,* Contemporary Press (This is a library resource book.)

The Eiffel Tower was completed in Paris on March 31, 1889.

86

Talking Walls

Talking Walls by Margy Burns Knight introduces young readers to different cultures by exploring walls around the world, from the Great Wall of China to the Berlin Wall. After sharing this book with your students, put up a large piece of butcher paper in the Social Studies Center. Encourage children to create their own "talking wall" by illustrating and writing about classroom events and topics of study. If you do this every month, you will eventually have a recorded history of your school year.

Globe Trotting

There is a wealth of literature that can take your students around the world and help them practice map skills in a fun way. As kids read any of the books listed below, have them locate the places visited on a map or globe. Or give each child a map and let him or her trace the journey. Oh, the places they'll go!

- *Away from Home* by Anita Lobel
- *Nine O'clock Lullaby* by Marilyn Singer
- *How to Make an Apple Pie and See the World* by Marjorie Priceman
- *The Spice Alphabet Book* by Jerry Pallotta
- *Whose Hat Is That?* by Brian and Rebecca Wildsmith
- *Amelia's Fantastic Flight* by Rose Bursik
- *This Is My House* by Arthur Dorros

Uno, Dos, Tres

Include the *Count Your Way* series by Jim Haskins in the Social Studies Center. These books introduce children to other cultures and teach them how to count to ten in other languages. Let kids practice counting with a friend and then teach the class.

Plan a Trip

Kids love finding out about their own community and state. Find a book that tells about favorite places for kids that are in or near your community. Place the book and a city or state map at the center, and let kids map out a Saturday adventure. This activity could blossom into a real plan for a family outing or a class field trip.

Once Upon a Time

Put fairy tales from around the world at the Social Studies Center for children to read or listen to on tape. They can compare and contrast the same tale from different countries or tell how the culture differs from their own. For example, use the many different variations of *Cinderella* listed below:

- *The Egyptian Cinderella* by Shirley Climo
- *The Day It Snowed Tortillas* by Joe Hayes
- *Yeh-Shen: A Cinderella Story from China* by Ai-Ling Louie
- *Moss Gown* by William Hooks

- *Mufaro's Beautiful Daughter: An African Tale* by John Steptoe
- *The Brocaded Slipper and Other Vietnamese Tales* by Lynette Dyer Vuong

88

Global Grab Bag

Find a large sturdy gift bag. Try to find one that has a "traveling" design, or glue a world map on the front. Add some ribbons and streamers and you're ready to go! Use the grab bag to introduce the study of another culture.

In the bag, place an assortment of objects that represent the culture. For example, if you are studying Australia, you could add some of the following objects: a stuffed kangaroo or koala, a jar of Vegemite, a boomerang, coral, an outback hat, a picture of Mem Fox, a prisoner's outfit, a sprig of eucalyptus, Australian postage stamps, coins, a map. Let students examine and discuss the items and tell how they are significant for the country.

Celebrate!

Have students research the origins of familiar holidays or investigate the celebrations of different cultures: Kwanzaa, Cinco de Mayo, Valentine's Day, Ground Hog's Day. They can make favors and decorations appropriate for the celebration or even plan activities the class can participate in.

Research Center

At the Research Center students can investigate subjects of personal interest and topics related to class theme units. Becoming proficient with resource materials will help students be more independent learners.

Materials

- ◆ atlas
- ◆ dictionary
- ◆ encyclopedia
- ◆ almanac
- ◆ maps and globe
- ◆ computer
- ◆ CD-ROM encyclopedia
- ◆ nonfiction books
- ◆ magazines
- ◆ newspaper articles
- • informative brochures
- ◆ photographs
- ◆ posters, charts
- ◆ paper
- ◆ pencils

Creative Teaching Press

Meaningful Materials

Survey children to find out their interests. This will help you stock the Research Center with meaningful materials for your students.

Research Rally

Consider your themes, and help students develop research options within a theme.

Bag It

Have kids decorate the front of a lunch bag to represent their research project. They can store any note cards in the bag until it's time to write the report. Younger children can make picture cards and do an oral report.

Mini-Investigations

Research projects don't always have to be serious topics or long and involved. Kids can do a mini-report on "How Bubble Gum Is Made" or "The Origins of Pizza."

■ ■ ■ ■ ■ ■ ■ ■ ■ ■
Research Center Quick Tips
■ ■ ■ ■ ■ ■ ■ ■ ■ ■

Have You Heard?

Consider having parents tape-record some research materials and short nonfiction books. This allows limited-English students and beginning readers to participate in research.

Inquiring Minds

Invite the children to develop questions they have about a specific topic. List the questions and post them at the Research Center.

Greetings, Researchers

Use greeting cards with realistic photos to spark interest in animal research. (Look for these cards at nature stores.) Add questions on the inside of the card.

Computer Research

Don't forget the computer connection when kids are doing research. Excellent source materials come on CD-ROMs and through the Internet.

Research Center Activities

K-W-L

Model for kids how to begin their research by using the K-W-L method. Make a three-door Flip-Flap Book (page 132), and label each section as shown. Students write the appropriate information on the inside of each flap. The K-W-L method would be the first step in any project at the Research Center.

K - What I Know About My Topic
W - What I Want to Know
L - What I Learned

What I Know about... Abe Lincoln	What I Want to Know about...	What I Learned about...
• President during Civil War • Very tall • Lawyer	What was he like as a boy?	• Went to school in one room. • Lived in a cabin • His mother died.

flip!

Facts from A to Z

Share, then place at the center, a variety of informative alphabet books from the library. Some choices are: *Alison's Zinnia* by Arnold Lobel, *ABC: The National Air and Space Museum* by Florence Mayers, *ABCedar: An Alphabet of Trees* by George Lyon, *Ashanti to Zulu* by Margaret Musgrove, and the series of ABC books by Jerry Pallotta. Have students choose a topic and research one related fact for every letter of the alphabet. Research can be done individually, with a partner, or in a small group. Young children can draw and cut out pictures for each page. Assemble the pages into a book.

Creative Teaching Press

Birthday Research

Provide books that give factual information about historical events for each day of the year. Have students research their birth date and create a book or time line showing the events that took place on that day.

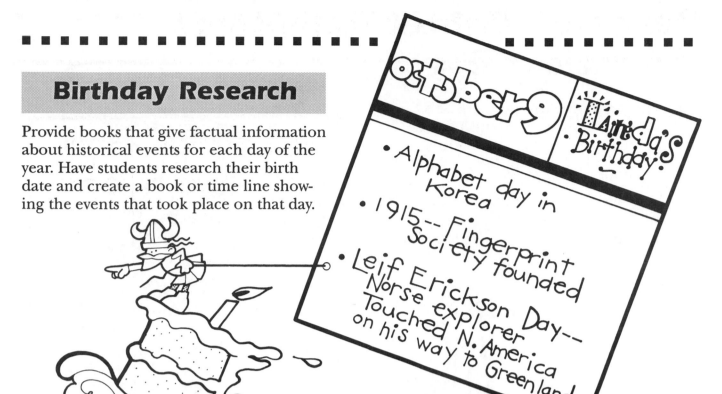

October 9 · Linda's Birthday

- Alphabet day in Korea
- 1915-- Fingerprint Society founded
- Leif Erickson Day-- Norse explorer Touched N. America on his way to Greenland

Books \ Inventions	Chocolate Chip Cookies	Band Aids
Mistakes That Worked	Invented in 1930 because Mrs. Wakefield ran out of baking chocolate. It was a delicious mistake!	
Steven Carey's Invention Book···	Mrs. Wakefield had a friend that read her new recipe on the radio! Everyone loved it!	Mr. Dicksen invented band aids because his wife always cut and burned herself!

Graphic Organizers

Show children how to use graphic organizers to organize the information they gather. Model this process with several different research topics before you turn students loose to work on their own. Kindergarten and first-grade teachers can continue this as a whole-group activity.

To make a quick and easy graphic organizer, fold unlined paper into 6–16 boxes, depending on the age of your students. Ask students to read several different sources and to make notes about (not copy word for word) the information they find.

Get on a Research Roll

Using adding machine tape to make a time line is a perfect way for students to show research information that is sequential. When the time line is complete, roll it up and put a rubber band around it. Place the research rolls into a bucket or box at the Research Center for other students to read, or display them on a bulletin board.

Conduct a Survey

Many researchers use surveys to collect data. Students can design a simple survey, interview classmates, compile the results, and record the information in a report or on a graph.

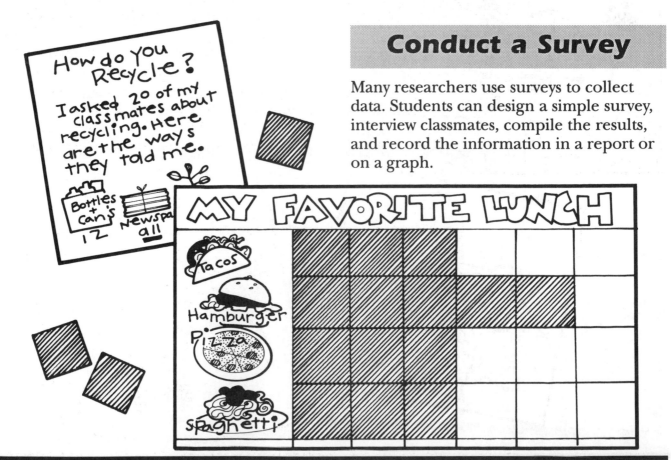

Creative Teaching Press

Travel Research

Students can research a famous place they would like to visit. Have them organize their information into a colorful travel brochure complete with illustrations highlighting the not-to-be-missed sights.

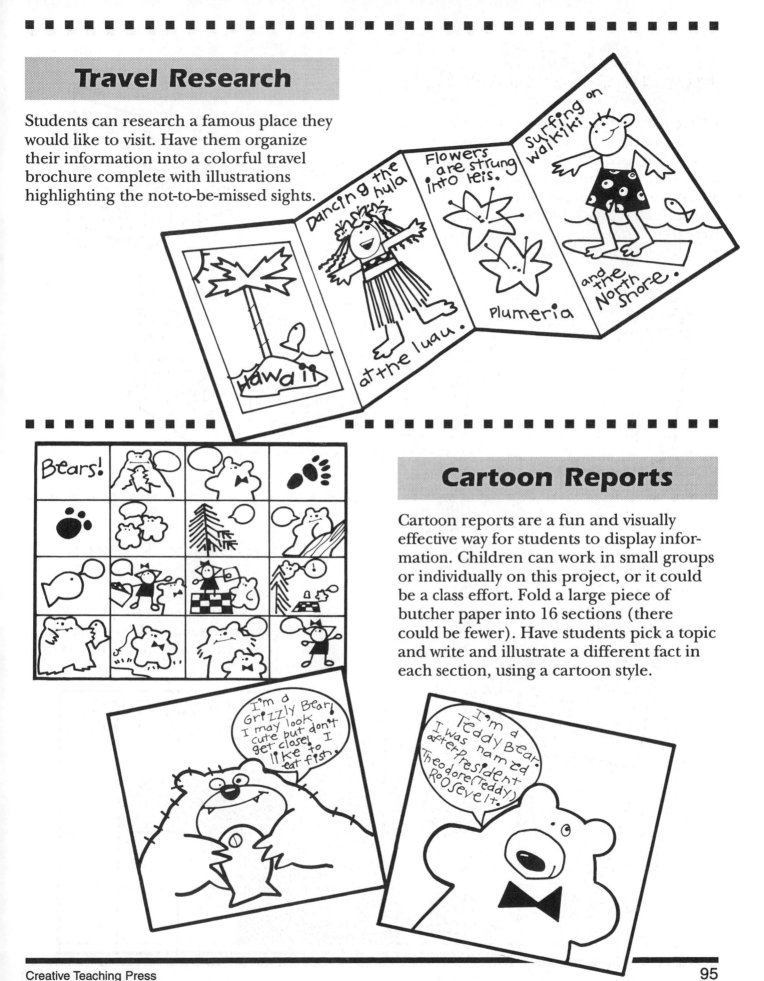

Cartoon Reports

Cartoon reports are a fun and visually effective way for students to display information. Children can work in small groups or individually on this project, or it could be a class effort. Fold a large piece of butcher paper into 16 sections (there could be fewer). Have students pick a topic and write and illustrate a different fact in each section, using a cartoon style.

Science Center

The Science Center should be a place where students can observe, hypothesize, investigate, and record their findings. Keep investigations simple enough for students to do independently. Students love to make discoveries on their own.

Materials

◆ collections (rocks, shells, insects, leaves)
◆ animals (aquarium, terrarium, ant farm)
◆ science books and magazines
◆ nests, bones, seeds, beans, plants
◆ batteries, wires, bulbs
◆ microscope and slides
◆ measuring materials
◆ scales
◆ magnifying glasses
◆ tweezers, tongs, eye droppers
◆ sponges
◆ containers (jars, bottles, cups)
◆ paper plates
◆ thermometers (indoor, outdoor)
◆ tubs
◆ clay
◆ wax paper, aluminum foil
◆ sorting trays
◆ science journals
◆ observation sheets

The Scientific Method

The Science Center is a natural place for the Scientific Method to be experienced firsthand. Post the steps on a chart (page 138).

Experiment of the Week

Each week (or month) introduce a different science investigation to the whole class. Invite students to do the experiment at the Science Center and record their observations and conclusions.

Gathering Materials

Let parent volunteers help you gather materials for science experiments. Send home a detailed list specifying materials and the date they are needed. You're more apt to do lots of investigations if you have help with preparation. (See page 139 for a form.)

Class Science Journal

Keep a class journal in the Science Center for kids to record observations, predictions, and results of ongoing activities.

Science Center Quick Tips

Scientist of the Week

Get a lab coat for the "Scientist of the Week" to wear as he or she oversees the Science Center. Possible responsibilities are: assist kids at the center, set up the weekly experiment, replenish supplies, act as a resource person.

Order Form

Students can use an order form (see page 140) to request materials for independent experiments. This will encourage them to use center resource books and give them choices in activities.

Guest Scientists

Invite parents and other guest scientists from your local community to introduce and model how to use some Science Center materials. Kids will line up to be first at the center.

Famous Scientists

Each month, feature a famous scientist such as Albert Einstein, Thomas Edison, Marie Curie, George Washington Carver, or Jonas Salk. Display appropriate reference books and, if possible, post photos.

Science Center Activities

When planning for the Science Center, choose activities from your required science curriculum and those that relate to current theme units. There are lots of library books that list experiments by topic. They ususally include a detailed list of materials needed and show how to do the experiment step by step. Post the materials and the steps on a chart at the center. The sample activities that follow will give you an idea of what kinds of activities would work well in a center setting.

Properties

This is an excellent activity to use at the beginning of the school year in your Science Center. It will help young scientists develop careful, accurate observation skills. Place different objects in the Science Center. Start with simple classroom objects such as books, pencils, or crayons. Later include natural objects such as shells, insects, leaves, or rocks.

Make a list of properties to look for when observing the objects: color, shape, size, texture, weight, smell. Brainstorm with students possible attributes for each property and place the list at the center. Ask students to select an object and to record as many possible observations as they can about the object. Add a magnifying glass for close-up observations. (See p. 141 for a sample observation form.)

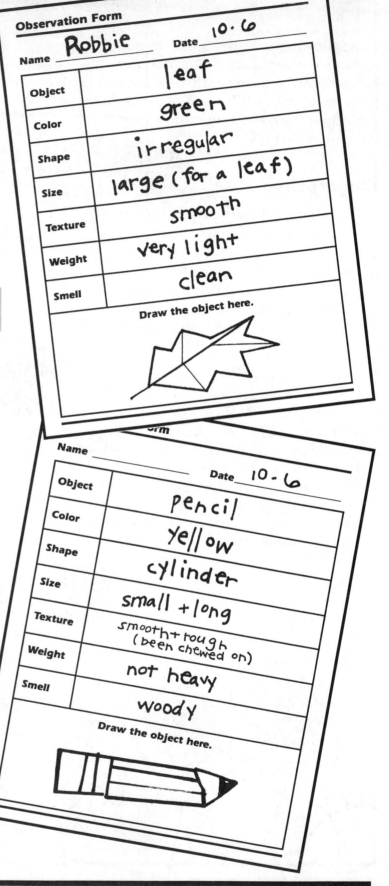

Observation Form

Name: Robbie   Date: 10·6

Object	leaf
Color	green
Shape	irregular
Size	large (for a leaf)
Texture	smooth
Weight	very light
Smell	clean

Draw the object here.

Name: _____   Date: 10-6

Object	pencil
Color	yellow
Shape	cylinder
Size	small + long
Texture	smooth + rough (been chewed on)
Weight	not heavy
Smell	woody

Draw the object here.

Magnifying Glasses

The following investigations are good examples of activities that can always be available to students throughout the school year. Children will discover something new each time they revisit the center.

Fingerprints

Taking fingerprints is easy. All you need is a black ink pad, unlined index cards, and some paper towels for cleanup. Show students how to roll their thumbs on the ink pad and then roll them carefully on the index card. Do the fingers the same way, and label the card with the child's name.

No two fingerprints are exactly alike, but all fingerprints are one of three basic types: The Loop—Lines start on one side, loop round the center, and end on the same side as they started. The Arch—Lines cross from side to side with a rise in the middle. The Whorl—Lines circle around the center point. Have students use a magnifying glass to sort and classify fingerprints. Provide examples of the three basic types.

For the Birds

How do birds stay dry? Have feathers available for children to do this simple investigation. Have students look at the feathers through a magnifying glass. They should notice that parts of the feather overlap. This overlapping helps keep water off. Invite students to use an eyedropper to drip water on the feather. What happens?

Bird nests are fun to examine, too. Students can inspect nests with a magnifying glass, list what building materials the bird used, and compare different kinds of nests.

Moldy Magnifying

Bring in a variety of moldy foods in clear baggies or clear plastic containers. Have students use the magnifying glass to look at the mold. Mold is a plant with roots and branches. Kids can compare the different kinds of molds on different foods.

Pumpkin Science

In the fall, bring pumpkins and books about pumpkins into your Science Center and invite students to try some of the following science investigations.

Pumpkins Are Plants

Kids can plant seeds and measure and record plant growth. Bring in different varieties of pumpkins, and ask students to compare the stems and leaves. Have them check pumpkin seed packets to find information about planting and rate of growth.

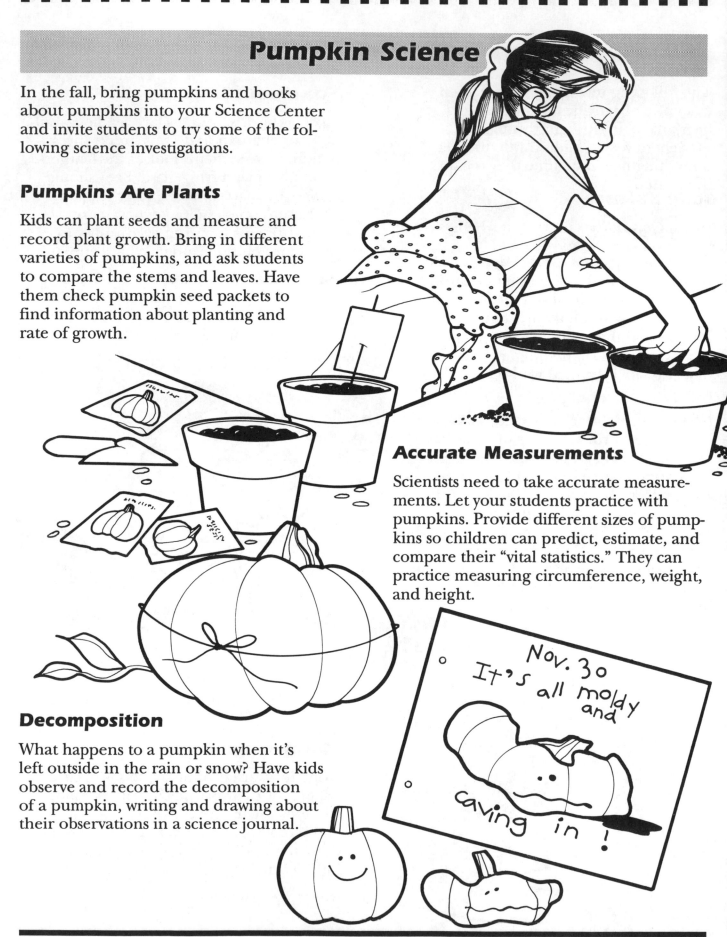

Accurate Measurements

Scientists need to take accurate measurements. Let your students practice with pumpkins. Provide different sizes of pumpkins so children can predict, estimate, and compare their "vital statistics." They can practice measuring circumference, weight, and height.

Decomposition

What happens to a pumpkin when it's left outside in the rain or snow? Have kids observe and record the decomposition of a pumpkin, writing and drawing about their observations in a science journal.

Nov. 30
It's all moldy and caving in!

Creative Teaching Press

Balance

Through balance activities, such as those that follow, students will make discoveries about the center of gravity, balancing points, and the force of gravity.

Body Balance

Challenge students to try and balance objects on various body parts. For example, they can balance a toothbrush, a pencil, a spoon, a plastic plate, or a ruler on one finger. Or they can balance larger items on their head, hand, or knee. They will need to adjust the position of an object and find its balancing point to stop it from tumbling off. Children can take pictures with a camera, draw pictures, or write about their observations and conclusions.

Can I Make It Balance?

Have kids cut a simple shape out of poster board and experiment to make it balance. For example, students can cut a "tightrope walker" and try to balance it on a piece of string as shown below. Or, they can cut a snake and make it balance on a finger. Provide small lumps of modeling clay that students can stick on the figure to get it to balance. Where did they put the clay? Why? (A hanging object balances when the center of gravity is directly below the balancing point.)

A Balancing Act

Students can make more discoveries about balancing points as they experiment with this activity. Secure a rolling pin to a table with modeling clay. Place a long tray on the rolling pin. Provide students with objects to balance. Challenge them with questions such as these: Will the tray balance without any objects? What objects will make the tray balance? Does it matter where you place the objects?

Computer Center

Since we live in the computer age, it's critical that students have an opportunity to practice computer skills and explore the wide variety of uses for the computer. Take the dustcover off, and let students have frequent access to your classroom computer.

Materials

- sturdy table or cart
- computer
- printer
- blank disks
- disk storage container
- labels
- mouse and mouse pad
- paper
- large poster-size picture of the keyboard
- commercial dustcover or sheet
- developmentally-appropriate software (page 105)
- chart that lists the names of available software
- class list

Creative Teaching Press

Setting Up

Place the computer near an outlet and away from high traffic areas, the sink, and any heat source such as windows or heaters. Tape down exposed cords with heavy tape.

Play It Safe

Keep magnets away from the computer and computer disks.

Monitoring Use

Situate the screen so that it can easily be seen from anywhere in the room. This will make it easier for the teacher to monitor use.

Computer Basics

Post directions on how to use the computer—turning it on, turning it off—as well as advice about when to stop and ask for help.

Computer Center Quick Tips

Time to Explore

Allow children to explore and discover capabilities of classroom software after they have learned the basics.

Quick Reference

Copy and laminate important pages from the program manual for reference when problems come up.

Working Together

Vary the number of children at the computer—one, two, or three. Students can take turns inputting information. "Watchers" will learn about the program as they observe and may be able to assist if there's a problem.

Personal Disks

Provide a disk for each child in your class. Students can store their work on their own personal disk.

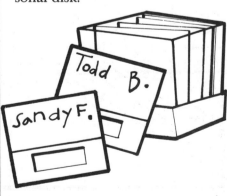

Computer Captains

Train Computer Captains who are experts on different software so that when children need help, they can go to the Captain and not to you.

Computer Art

If students don't have typing skills, you may want them to create a picture on the computer and do their writing at the Writing Center.

On Display

Don't forget to put a bulletin board up in the center so kids can display the work they have done on the computer.

Ongoing Story

Set up an ongoing story. Type the story beginning, then have each child add to it. Periodically print out the story, and post it on the Computer Center bulletin board.

More Computer Center Quick Tips

In the News

Set up a newsletter template on the computer, and have each child type in a newsworthy bit of information each week or month.

Add-A-Fact

When involved with a unit of study, have kids type in facts they have learned about the theme. Using a large font, periodically print out and post the list. Students can also make a list of questions for classmates to answer.

High-Tech Help

Consider investing in a computer-to-TV connector. You'll be able to demonstrate new programs to the whole class at one time. Whatever is on the computer monitor is projected on the TV screen.

Keep Current

To keep current on the many possibilities for using computers in the classroom, computer instructional strategies, and new products, subscribe to a professional magazine such as *Electronic Learning Magazine,* Scholastic (1-800-544-2917).

Creative Teaching Press

Computer Software

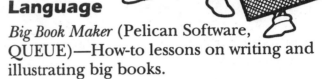

It's important to use software that is developmentally-appropriate for your students. The following programs are of high quality and are appropriate for use in K-3 classrooms. (Check to see which programs are compatible with your classroom computer.) New software is constantly being offered and updated, so it's a good idea to subscribe to resources that evaluate new software. Three good resource titles are also listed below.

Integrated Programs

ClarisWorks (Claris).
Microsoft Works (Microsoft).

Keyboarding

Kid Keys (Davidson).

Creativity Programs

Kid Pix 2 (Broderbund)—Drawing program.
The Print Shop (Broderbund) and *Super Print* (Scholastic)—Create signs, banners, cards, etc. Includes graphics.

Math and Science

The Graph Club (Tom Snyder Productions)—Ways to collect, sort, and analyze information.
James Discovers Math (Broderbund)—Measurement, time, songs, and rhymes.
The Magic School Bus (Microsoft)—A version of the famous book series.
Millie's Math House (Edmark)—Shapes and sizes, number recognition, and counting.
Thinking Things (Edmark)—Math problem solving and brain building.

Language

Big Book Maker (Pelican Software, QUEUE)—How-to lessons on writing and illustrating big books.
Explore a Story (William K. Bradford)—Animated, audio-ability to isolate a word and hear the word.
Kids Words 2 (Davidson)—Introduction to authoring.
The Living Books (series) (Broderbund)—Animated picture books.
Storybook Weaver (MECC)—Students create a scene and write a story.

Three excellent sources for information on new software are:

Children's Software Revue
(Newsletter rates software.)
520 N. Adams Street
Ypsilanti, MI 48197
1-800-993-9499

Hi-Scope Buyers Guide
to Children's Software
(Annual survey of software.)
600 N. River Street
Ypsilanti, MI 48198
1-800-407-7377

Children's Software
(Quarterly newsletter.)
720 Kuhlman
Houston, TX 77024
1-800-556-5590

K/1 Theme Center: The Farm

These sample center activities will show you how a farm theme can be integrated into various centers in kindergarten and first-grade classrooms. Use this general format to create centers for any theme your class is studying.

Materials

- nonfiction and fiction books related to the theme
- straw hat, overalls, bandanna
- toy tractors, trucks, farm machinery, tools
- plastic or student-made farm animals
- appliance boxes to make farm animals, fences, and a barn
- straw, hay bales
- seeds to "plant"
- farm stickers
- farm animal-shape notepads
- farm animal sounds on tape
- rubber stamps with farm theme

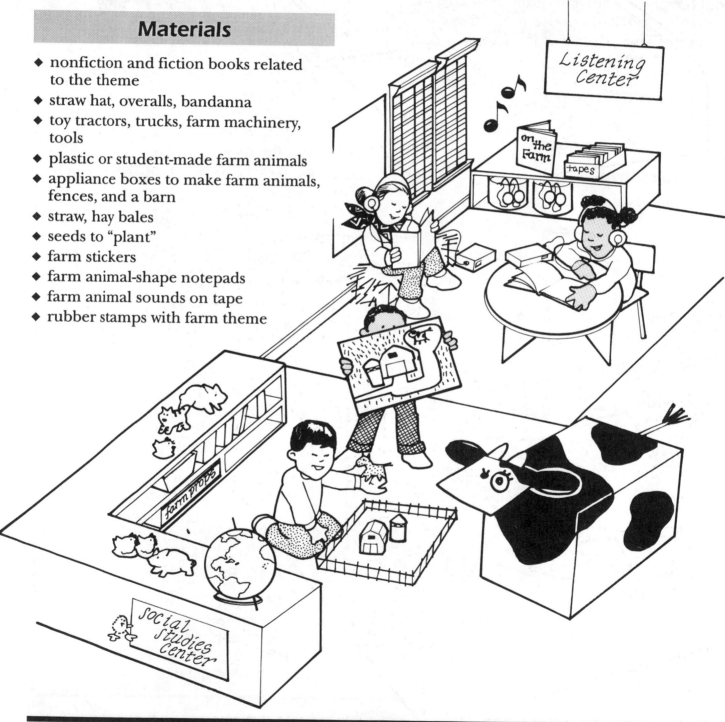

Creative Teaching Press

Writing Center

tractor (Tricia)
cow (Ben) barn (Joey) farmer (Tyler)
horse (Aubree)

Dramatic Play Center

Mrs. Holliman

Reading Center

Science Center

one, two

theme center

Dramatic Play Center

Set up a mini-farm in the Dramatic Play Center complete with stuffed farm animals that children have brought from home, a pretend garden with a hoe and vegetables, a wheelbarrow, a bucket and stool for "milking" cows. Students can plant and harvest crops, feed the animals, build fences with blocks, and feed the farmhands. Provide farm clothes such as overalls, straw hats, bandannas, and rubber boots so students can dress the part.

Listening Center

Look for commercial tapes of farm sounds and farm songs. Tape farm stories and place the book at the center so students can follow along. Invite students to tape their favorite stories complete with farm animal sound effects.

Creative Teaching Press

Writing Center

With students, brainstorm farm-related words, and post them on a chart at the Writing Center. (If you write the child's name under "their word," they will remember it and can read it to others.) Students can use this word bank for writing activities such as those described below.

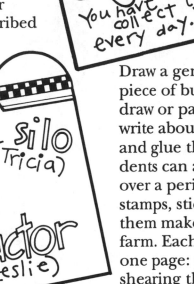

You have to collect eggs every day.

shearing the sheep

Farm Words

cow (Ben)

barn (Joe)

silo (Tricia)

horse (Aubree)

tractor (Leslie)

Draw a general farm scene on a large piece of butcher paper. Let each student draw or paint a farm animal and label or write about their animal. Cut these out and glue them on the farm scene. Students can also write a farm counting book over a period of several days, using farm stamps, stickers, or drawings. Or have them make a class book about jobs on the farm. Each child can write and illustrate one page: planting seeds, collecting eggs, shearing the sheep, etc.

Reading Center

Create a cozy hayloft reading area. Bring in some hay bales from your local feed or garden store. Add a good selection of books, stuffed farm animals, and cozy quilts. Write theme-related poems on charts. Place the books and poems in a "trough" (box or basket) so students can pick and choose. Write lyrics from farm songs on sentence strips, and place them in a pocket chart. Students can read and sing "Old MacDonald" and other songs as they track lyrics with a pointer.

Math Center

Collect small plastic farm animals to use as manipulatives in the Math Center. Make animal pens out of lunch bags (see illustration). These paper bag pens can be used along with manipulatives for counting, addition, and subtraction activities and for writing and solving story problems.

Let students use theme-related rubber stamps to record math problems and to print patterns. Have the children use felt shapes on a flannel board to make farm animals and buildings. Students can use different lengths of rope or plastic farm animals as nonstandard units of measure. For example, ask students to find out how many cows will fit across a desk. Or challenge them to find something smaller than, larger than, or the same size as the piece of rope.

Science Center

Collect seed packets. Students can sort and classify different kinds of seeds. They can plant different seeds and see that each seed produces its own unique plant. They can measure plant growth. If you extend this center outside, they may even be able to harvest vegetables. If you have access to an incubator, you can hatch baby chicks.

110

Social Studies Center

Let students create a farm scene using plastic farm animals and buildings. Ask them to draw a map of their farm. Include books on different kinds of farms: dairy farms, poultry farms, vegetable farms, fruit farms, wheat farms, etc. Students can paint different farm murals or research and report on the different farms.

Cut out food pictures from magazines, and place them at the center. Let students figure out what farm animal or farm product the food came from. For example, bread comes from wheat, butter comes from milk which comes from a cow, etc.

Cooking Center

Let students make butter at the Cooking Center. Provide each child with a baby food jar with a tight lid. Fill each jar half-full with cream, and have students shake the jar vigorously until butter forms. Pour off the liquid, and spread the butter on crackers for a tasty treat. If you can, bring in an old-fashioned butter churn for students to see.

2/3 Theme Center: The Ocean

These sample center activities will show you how an ocean theme can be integrated into various centers in second and third grade classrooms. Use this general format to create centers for any theme your class is studying.

Materials

- nonfiction and fictions books related to the theme
- theme-related magazine and newspaper articles
- sailor, captain, and pirate hats
- ocean stickers
- notepads shaped like ocean creatures
- sea creature sounds on tape
- ocean manipulatives such as seashells, and plastic fish
- rubber stamps with an ocean theme
- globe with oceans marked
- information about "ocean" careers (sailor, oceanographer, marine biologist)
- shell collection

Creative Teaching Press

Reading Center

Have students paint a surfing mural and title it "Catch the Reading Wave" to display on the wall or the back of a bookshelf. Provide fiction and nonfiction books, magazine articles, and brochures on topics related to an ocean theme. Add comfortable beach chairs, an umbrella, and beach towels. Have students keep track of the books they read during this unit of study in reading logs decorated with an ocean motif.

Writing Center

The props for the Writing Center might include a sailor hat, a captain hat, and a pirate hat. Use blue paper, stationery with a ship motif, and notepads shaped like ocean creatures for writing activities. Let students make their own stationery with rubber stamps or stickers. Brainstorm lists of theme-related words and writing topics to post at the center. Keep adding to these lists throughout the unit of study. Encourage students to write about their own experiences at the ocean.

Creative Teaching Press

Research Center

Survey your class and list ocean research topics students might want to pursue such as endangered marine life, ship building, famous ships and captains, the Vikings, and whales. Stock this center with books on these topics. Invite children to bring books and resources from home. Give students a variety of ways to show what they have learned from their research. See page 138 for a list of options.

Listening Center

Tape-record nonfiction material so students can listen and do research. This will be a real benefit for students with limited reading skills. Consider taping one or two chapters a week of a novel. Students can listen to a new part of the story each week.

Math Center

Collect shells and small plastic sea creatures for students to use as manipulatives for solving problems. Students can record addition, subtraction, or multiplication problems using ocean creature rubber stamps. They can use real shells to build and extend patterns or stamp sea-life patterns on strips of paper. *Sea Squares* by Joy Hulme is an excellent literature connection for this center. The delightful sea creatures in this book lead students from counting into multiplication.

Science Center

Place seashells and books on shells at the center. Ask students to use the books to identify the different kinds of shells. Children can label the shells for a class shell collection. Students can also sort models or pictures of sea life by type, such as mollusk, fish, crustacean, and mammal.

Challenge students to design their own boat. It must be strong enough to hold a marble (or other small object) and still float. Provide an assortment of common objects for boat building such as foil, paper, plastic cups, cardboard, and craft sticks. Students could also test the boats to see how much weight they can hold before sinking.

...Indian Ocean

Social Studies Center

Place a globe in the center, and have students identify the oceans of the world. Have students keep a glossary of theme-related geographical terms such as *island, archipelago, peninsula, reef, harbor, inlet, cove,* and *bay.* Challenge them to identify these landforms on maps.

With the children make a list of "ocean" careers such as sailor, oceanographer, marine biologist, etc. Students can research these careers and share the information with the class.

116

Poetry Center

Collect poems about the ocean and ocean animals. Mount, laminate, and display them at the center. Record some poems on tape with nautical music playing in the background. Have students help make a poetry bulletin board as pictured. Each child can write a favorite or original poem in the center of a paper plate with a black border. Glue this "port hole poetry" on a large butcher paper ship named the USS Rhyme.

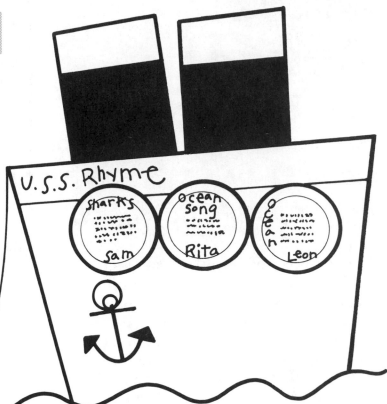

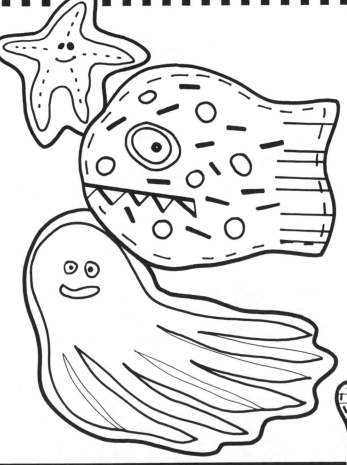

Art Center

Crayon-resists are perfect for an ocean theme. Have students create their ocean picture with crayon and paint over it with blue watercolor paint. Or invite them to make giant stuffed ocean creatures. Students paint or color their favorite ocean creature on a large double piece of butcher paper. After both pieces are cut out, they staple around the edge of the creature, leaving an opening. Have them stuff their creature with newsprint or tissue and staple it closed. These sea creatures look great on an ocean mural, hung from the ceiling, or displayed on a fishnet on the wall.

More Center Solutions

This section offers additional ideas for centers. Do not consider this a definitive list. You and your students will probably come up with lots of new center ideas that meet the needs of your class.

Dramatic Play Center

Think of the dramatic play area as a place children can "act out" their real world. The house center is a good start, but change the focus of this center on a regular basis. Consider setting up some of the following centers throughout the year: school, restaurant, gas station, bank, fire or police station, hospital, doctor's or dentist's office, post office, zoo, art gallery, beauty salon, theater, toy store, airport, grocery store.

Whenever possible, stock your Dramatic Play Center with the "real thing" rather than toy props. Garage sales and thrift stores are great sources of inexpensive materials. Send home a wish list to parents, or visit local businesses and ask for donations. For example, your local bank might donate deposit slips, and travel agencies might provide outdated brochures. Be sure to include appropriate books in the center to provide information kids need to get the "job" done.

For successful dramatic play experiences, introduce the center by talking about children's related personal experiences. Also introduce the various props and talk about their uses. For example, discuss what happens at the vet's office and who works there. Children can treat sick animals, read about animals and pet care products, make signs, handle money, and give customers information about their pets. Stuffed animals that children have brought from home may act as pets.

The Doctor is in

Museum Center

Have older students design a museum that highlights current theme units or topics of study. For example, if you are studying mammals, students can set up a natural history museum with information, illustrations, and student projects on display.

Valuable research and application of life skills take place when children are involved in this kind of activity. They are reading, writing, and working cooperatively to design and create the museum. Depending on their personal research, they are creating projects, displays, videos, and interviews that will become part of the museum. Invitations for a guided tour of the museum can be designed and sent to other classes.

Invention Center

This center is great for all that "junk" you have collected over the years such as wood scraps, egg cartons, margarine tubs, and cardboard tubes. Children can come up with some incredible ideas and inventions such as a pencil organizer made out of tubs and toilet paper tubes, or a paint jar with its own drip control sponge.

Projects can be done individually or as a cooperative effort. Make sure children have the opportunity to share their inventions with the rest of the class. *Invention Book* by Steven Caney and *Mistakes That Worked* by Charlotte Foltz Jones are both good books to include at this center.

Overhead Projector Center

Set up the overhead projector in a private corner. For a screen, tape a piece of white paper on the side of a file cabinet or on the back of a bookshelf. Buy a box of transparencies—they come clear and in colors. Or, collect laminating scraps from the trash. The following list of possible activities will get you started:

◆ Let kids write and illustrate their own original transparency stories. Store them in clear plastic sleeves and put them in a three-ring binder for classmates to use at the center. You can schedule a special story time so that authors can share their creations with a small group.

◆ Make a True/False work mat on a large transparency. Write teacher- or student-generated statements (some true, others false) on small transparency squares. Coordinate them with your theme or unit of study. Let students sort statements into True/False categories on the overhead.

◆ Historical events can be sequenced on the overhead. Write dates and events on transparency squares for children to sequence.

◆ Young students can match color words and colors, upper- and lower-case letters, and numbers with sets and number words.

◆ Have students use transparent manipulatives made with rubber stamps (see page 78 for directions) to create rebus stories written on overhead transparencies.

Block and Construction Center

Blocks are for ALL ages . . . yes, even first, second, and third graders! Use blocks to bridge curriculum areas. Students can build a 3-D map of their community or measure the area and perimeter of their constructions. They can explore structural engineering by testing the stability of the buildings. They can use blocks to build simple machines such as levers, pulleys, or rollers.

Don't forget to include small construction sets such as Legos, Lincoln Logs, and Bristle Blocks. Garage sales are a good source for inexpensive construction materials. Record buildings and constructions by photographing them or by having children draw pictures. Put them all together and create your own class *Architectural Digest.*

Put hard hats in the center to indicate how many children can be in the Block Center at one time. Store blocks in tubs, boxes, baskets, and on shelves. Mark them so that children know exactly where the blocks are to be returned. This will make life easier for you and for the children. Remember to give children of all ages time to explore with the blocks and construction materials. They need to "get to know the materials" before they begin serious construction.

Word Center

Introduce this center with the book *Donovan's Word Jar* by Mona Lisa deGross, a story of a little boy who collects words. Make a word jar out of a gallon jar and place a variety of dictionaries and a thesaurus at the center. Encourage students to collect words for the jar. They can write the word and the definition on a slip of paper and add it to the jar. At the end of the week, the class can go through the word jar and learn many new words together.

This center can also give children the opportunity to add to their own personal word banks. A great way to organize a word bank is to use a 3" x 5" file box, alphabetical dividers, and unlined index cards.

For a motivating way to practice spelling, have children choose challenging words from their writing pieces, theme study, or research. They practice spelling and writing the words in a variety of interesting ways: on a typewriter, with alphabet stamps, with colored markers or disappearing ink, in a sand tray, or on a tray squirted with a layer of shaving cream.

Fine Motor Center

Fine motor skills aren't just for young children. Older children need to work on these skills too. Many have excellent "thumb skills" from playing Nintendo, but don't forget their fingers need a good workout. Alternate different activities throughout the year:

- working with modeling clay
- using tweezers to pick up nuts, seeds, crayons
- using chopsticks or tongs to pick up larger objects
- sewing (tapestry needle sewing on Styrofoam trays, cross stitch)
- paper tearing
- weaving or lacing

Creative Teaching Press

Sorting Center

Try a sorting center. The preparation is easy, and any curriculum area can be represented. Keep the center up throughout the year by periodically changing the items to be sorted. Sort seashells for an ocean theme, sort coins for math, sort pasta after reading *Strega Nona,* and sort rocks when studying earth science. The possibilities are endless!

You'll need containers for sorting. Tubs, plastic microwave trays, and old place mats work well for larger objects. Egg cartons, muffin tins, and ice-cube trays work well for smaller items such as seeds, pebbles, pasta, or beads. Students can also sort objects on a large laminated Venn diagram. Ask students to help you collect items to be sorted.

It's a good idea to brainstorm sorting attributes with the class each time you put out a new sorting material. Post the list at the center. Or have kids sort using their own criteria, and let other students observe and determine what criteria were used.

Box and Can Center

Children can investigate food boxes and cans for information instead of using workbooks or skill sheets. Create a list of generic questions that will work with boxes and cans. The following will give you a start:

- ◆ What geometric shapes can you find on the box?
- ◆ How many vitamins (minerals) are in this product?
- ◆ How many descriptive words can you find?
- ◆ How much does the package weigh?
- ◆ How many servings are there?
- ◆ What is the fat (protein, carbohydrate) content?
- ◆ What is the price per ounce/pound?

Cooking Center

Don't let this one scare you! There are lots of books out there with recipes for snacks that require no hot plate, microwave, oven, or electric frying pan. This may be one of those centers that is not up all the time. You can save it for special events. That's okay—the important thing is to cook with your kids.

A Cooking Center offers many benefits. Students can practice math and reading skills in a meaningful way, learn science concepts as they discover the physical and chemical changes that take place during cooking, and develop good work habits as they carefully follow directions in sequential order. They'll have fun while learning an important life skill.

Set up the center near a sink. Write the recipe on a large chart (add pictures for young readers), and place the utensils and ingredients for the featured recipe in a tub or box. Post lists of safety and cleanup rules too. Have students cook with a partner or in a small group. You may also feel more comfortable if you have a parent volunteer helping with this center.

It's not hard to collect cooking utensils. Parents often have items to donate, and garage sales are an inexpensive source. To save yourself time outside the classroom, enlist the help of a "volunteer shopper" to purchase and deliver the ingredients to the classroom.

Puzzles and Games

This is an easy center that can be up all year long. Just change the games periodically. Garage sales and donations from parents will help you stock the center. Children can problem-solve, work cooperatively, and practice a variety of other skills depending on the games available.

Have a large jigsaw puzzle out at all times. Model different strategies students can use to assemble the puzzle such as using color, shape, and size clues. Students can add a few pieces whenever they have a few spare minutes. Other items for this center include:

- ◆ strategy games such as checkers, chess, or backgammon
- ◆ brain-teaser puzzles that students can solve with a friend
- ◆ 3-D manipulative puzzles
- ◆ parquetry blocks and patterns
- ◆ secret codes
- ◆ mystery-solving games
- ◆ word games like Scrabble, Pictionary, Boggle
- ◆ math games like dominoes or Yahtzee
- ◆ cryptograms
- ◆ word jumbles
- ◆ crossword puzzles
- ◆ giant floor jigsaw puzzles

Look and Learn Center

This is another versatile center. Students can practice or apply skills from any curriculum area. Make the "Look and Learn" grid as shown below on a bulletin board, a piece of plywood, or poster board. (For kindergarten, you might want to make a smaller grid. Four to eight boxes would be enough.) Draw up and reproduce a student response sheet to match the grid. (A sample grid is on page 142.) You will need to put Velcro, pushpins, or hooks in each square so the cards can be hung on the board.

Write math problems, science questions, language arts skills, etc. on index cards. Place a card in some of the boxes on the grid. (Stick a small piece of Velcro on the back of each card, or punch a small hole to hang the card.) Leave some squares empty. Students can read the question, problem, or task on the "Look and Learn" board and write their response in the corresponding box on the matching response sheet.

Look and Learn Grid

Student Answer Sheet

Look and Learn Grid

Student Answer Sheet

Reproducibles

Center Activity Planning Sheet

Center

Date

Objective(s)

Activity

Materials

Evaluation

Creative Teaching Press

All-Purpose Checklist

Picture Directions

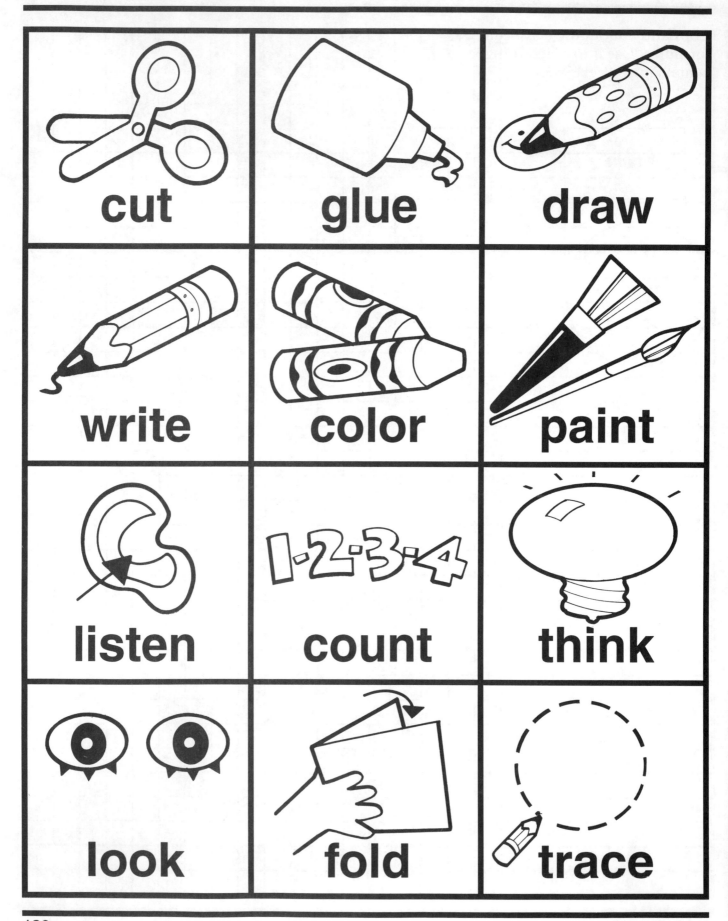

cut

glue

draw

write

color

paint

listen

count

think

look

fold

trace

Room Arranger

Copy and cut out the classroom furniture. Use it to help arrange centers in your classroom.

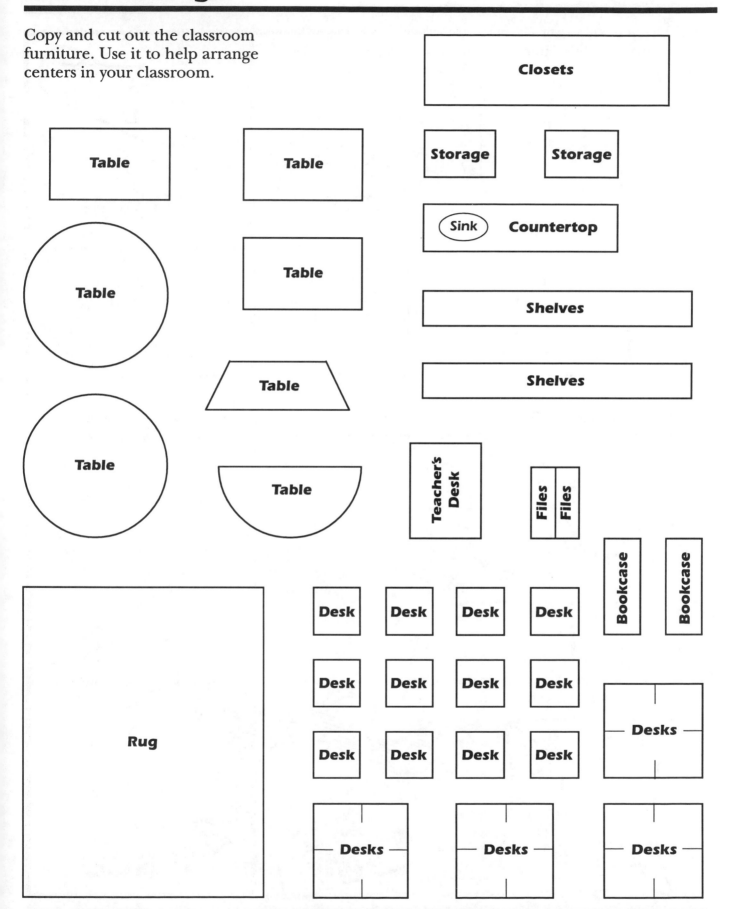

Flip-Flap Book

1. Fold a sheet of paper (9" x 12" or 12" x 18") into eighths. Open and cut to center fold as shown.

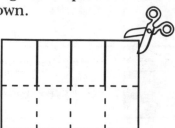

2. Fold cut pieces down at center fold. Crease.

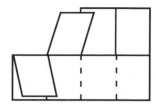

3. Students write and illustrate on and under the flaps.

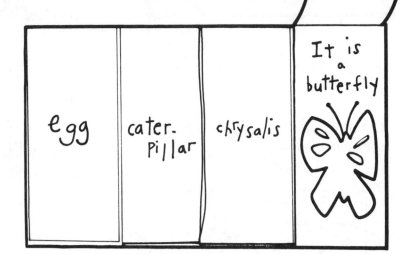

egg | cater-pillar | chrysalis | It is a butterfly

Paper Bag Book

1. Hold the bag with the flap towards you. Fold the open end up under the flap.

2. Open the bag and staple the completed story pages below the fold line.

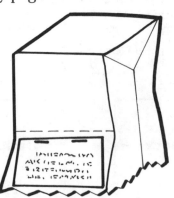

3. Draw and cut out a suitable illustration and glue it to the flap of the bag. Use construction paper scraps to add parts of the body.

4. Fold up the bottom half under the flap, and write the title of the book and the author's name.

Monkey Business by Sally

Creative Teaching Press

Pop-Up Book

1. Fold a sheet of construction paper (9" x 12" or 12" x 18") in half.

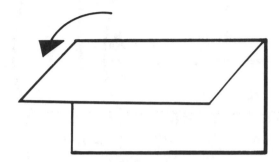

2. Open the paper and draw a background scene on the top half.

3. Make a tab by cutting two slits, one inch apart, on the fold. Push the tab through to the inside of the folded page. You can make more than one tab.

4. On another piece of paper draw the object you want to pop up. Glue it on the tab as shown.

5. Write on the bottom portion of the page.

6. Glue the completed pages together as shown to make a book.

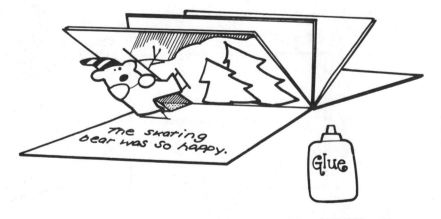

Poof Book

1. Fold the paper in half widthwise. Then fold it once more in the same direction.

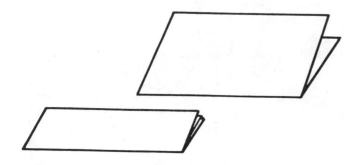

2. Fold the paper in half in the opposite direction.

3. Open to a half sheet. Starting from the folded edge, cut along the crease. Stop where the fold lines intersect.

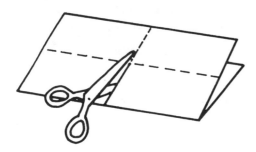

4. Open the paper completely.

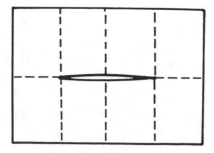

5. Fold paper lengthwise.

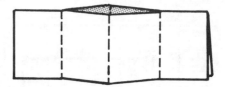

6. Grasp the outer edges as shown, and push them towards the center. The opening should "poof" out. Keep pushing until a book of four sections is formed.

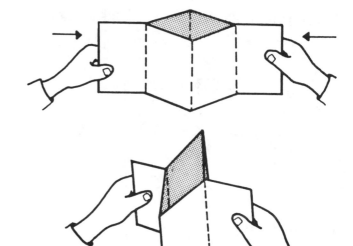

7. Fold the pages closed, and write the title of the book and the author's name on the cover.

Creative Teaching Press

Person Book

1. Fold a piece of 12" x 18" construction paper into eight equal sections as shown.

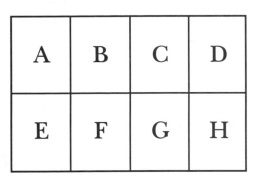

2. Cut out sections E and H.

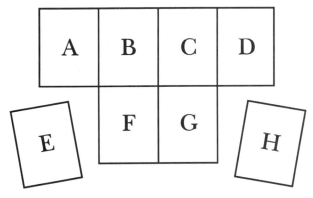

3. Cut a head from another piece of construction paper. Glue it to the top of sections B and C.

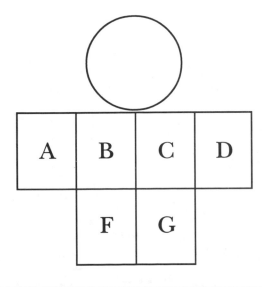

4. Draw a face; add hair and clothing. Add hands and shoes cut from paper scraps.

5. Write in sections B and C, or add as many pages as needed.

Special Specs Pattern

Color and cut out. Glue where indicated.

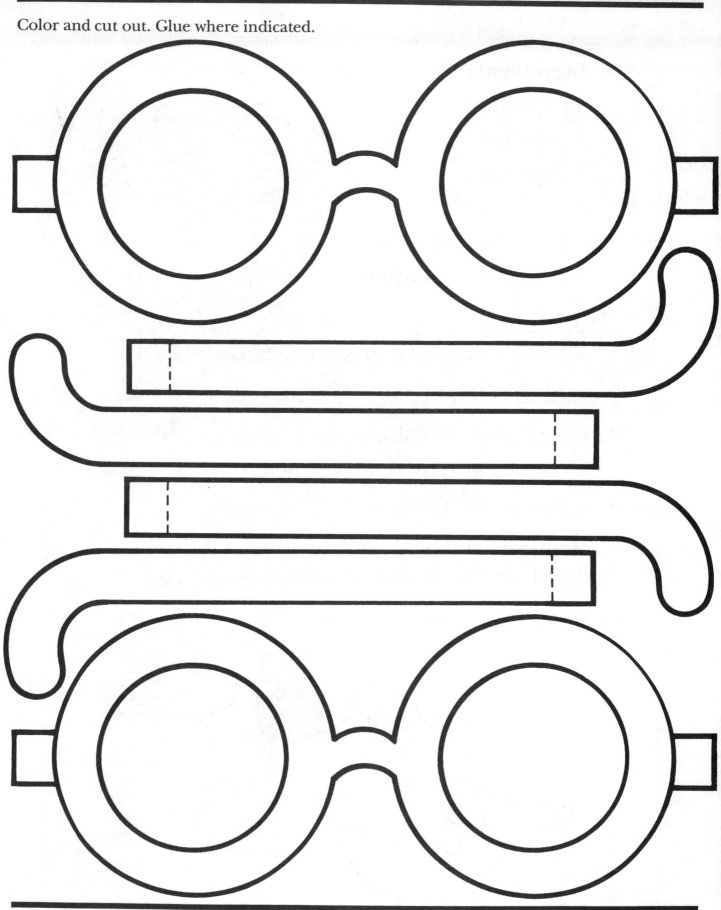

Playdough Recipe

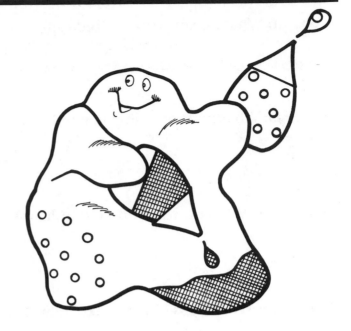

Ingredients

4 cups flour

2 cups salt

4 cups water

4 T. oil

8 tsp. cream of tartar

desired food coloring

1. Mix together dry ingredients in a saucepan.

2. Add the oil and mix.

3. Combine food coloring and water and add to the other ingredients.

4. Cook on low heat for 3–5 minutes.

5. Remove from heat onto floured board and knead to desired consistency.

6. Keep in a covered container.

Scientific Method

Problem: What do you want to find out?

Materials: What materials do you need?

Hypothesis: What do you think might happen?

Procedure: What steps did you take to find out?

Conclusion: What did you find out? Was it what you thought would happen?

Student Response Options

Give a
Speech
Mock Interview
Taped Presentation
Puppet Show

Do a(n)
Experiment
Dramatization
Demonstration
Performance

Write a(n)
Book
Newspaper/Magazine Article
Journal Entry
ABC Book
Poem
Advertisement

Make a(n)
Art Project
Bulletin Board
Display
Poster
Time Line
Brochure
Graph
Chart

Parent Science Letter

Dear Parent(s),

We love doing science experiments and investigations in the Science Center, and we need your help gathering some consumable materials. I hope you can help out by sending the following items. We need them by _____.

_____   _____

_____   _____

_____   _____

Thank you for supporting our budding scientists.

_____

Order Form for Science Materials

_____
date

Dear _____,
     teacher's name

I would like to do a science experiment on _____

_____ .

I need the following materials:

_____   _____

_____   _____

_____   _____

_____   _____

Thanks. Science is fun!

_____
student's name

Creative Teaching Press

Observation Form

Name _____ **Date**_____

Object	
Color	
Shape	
Size	
Texture	
Weight	
Smell	

Draw the object here.

LOOK AND LEARN